GREAT
CANADIA
WOMEN

Nineteen Portraits of Extraordinary Women

Lisa Wojna

FOLK
LORE
PUBLISHING

The Publisher: Folklore Publishing
Website: www.folklorepublishing.com

Library and Archives Canada Cataloguing in Publication

Wojna, Lisa, 1962–
   Great Canadian women : nineteen portraits of extraordinary
   women / Lisa Wojna.

(Great Canadian stories)
Includes bibliographical references.
ISBN 13: 978-1-894864-47-3
ISBN 10: 1-894864-47-6

   1. Women—Canada—Biography. I. Title. II. Series.

FC26.W6W63 2005   920.72'0971   C2005-904720-8

Project Director: Faye Boer
Project Editor: Kathy van Denderen
Production: Trina Koscielnuk
Cover Image: Silken Lauman. Courtesy of CP/Canadian Olympic Com-
mittee (Ted Grant)
Title Page Image: Nellie McClung. Courtesy of Glenbow Archives, NC-6-1311

We acknowledge the support of the Alberta Foundation for the Arts
for our publishing program.

We acknowledge the support of the Canada Council for our publishing
program.

PC: P5

Canada Council   Conseil des Arts
for the Arts   du Canada

Contents

❧✢❧

Dedication

*To Melissa and Jada—my two Great Canadian
Women of the future.*

Acknowledgements

I THANK THOSE INDIVIDUALS WHO TOOK THE TIME TO respond to my e-mails, check facts, or provide more information. Your efforts fleshed out several stories. To Greg Ellis and the Galt Museum in Lethbridge, Alberta, whose staff went all-out to provide information and newspaper articles on Anne Campbell. Without their efforts, there would be no story on this fine woman since, despite the fact she is a local hero in her own right, not much has been written about her. Thank you to the staff of the Wetaskiwin Public Library—your help was invaluable. Special thanks to Faye Boer of Folklore Publishing. Her enthusiasm for this series is a constant inspiration—and very contagious. Thanks to my editor Kathy van Denderen for her valued insights and sharp eye that brought this manuscript from a work in progress to completion. It's a true pleasure working with these two fine women. As always, to my children—Peter, Melissa, Matthew and Nathan—they are a constant inspiration to me. And finally, thank you to my husband, Garry. His support, willingness to help and the seemingly endless amount of patience and understanding he doles out to me on a regular basis is always appreciated and never taken for granted.

~⚬✕⚬~

Introduction

The purpose of woman's life is just the same as the purpose of man's life—that she may make the best possible contribution to the generation in which she is living.

–Louise Crummy McKinney

BORN ON SEPTEMBER 22, 1868, LOUISE CRUMMY MCKINNEY was a woman of extraordinary foresight. Her numerous accomplishments include the organizing of the Women's Christian Temperance Union in 1905 where for a time she also served as president both provincially and nationwide. She was the first woman elected to a provincial legislature in the British Empire, and was one of five Canadian women—known as the Famous Five—who fought for the right for women to be considered "persons" under the law.

Although she recognized the value of a woman's role in the home, McKinney said her life "has never been bounded by the four walls of a home. I have always been interested in affairs of church and state." For McKinney and other women like her, the world offered endless adventures and wondrous opportunities—if only they were allowed to partake of them. Many doors were closed to women simply because of their gender, and it would take the strong-mindedness, persistence and endless courage of women like those profiled in this collection to pave the way for equal rights between the sexes.

It wasn't until May 19, 1919, when the United States government passed the 19th amendment to the U.S. Constitution that gave women in that country the right to vote. Here in Canada, that same right was afforded to women first in the province of Manitoba in 1916. And it wasn't until 10 years later, in 1929, that women were recognized as "persons" under the law.

Gaining acceptance as "persons" seems absurd, even for a time before the feminist revolution. Yet that milestone was only the beginning. Women still had barriers to conquer if they were to follow their hearts into anything remotely deemed a man's territory. Today, we tell our youngsters to follow their dreams—anything can be attained with hard work and perseverance. At the turn of the 20th century, women still had to fight to gain acceptance as doctors, though they may have graduated with higher grades than their male counterparts.

While it's not uncommon for a woman to pilot a plane today, women who'd earned their wings back in the 1930s were thought of as silly for their efforts. According to C.G. Grey, editor of the British publication *Aeroplan*, women who thought they had what it took to shuttle planes from place to place during World War II were fooling themselves. Pilot's licence or not, it was clear this kind of woman didn't even possess "the intelligence to scrub the floor of a hospital properly or...can't cook her husband's dinner."

Despite the obstacles, many of which were mountainous, or the narrow-minded opinions of outspoken commentators, Canadian women fought to follow their callings. That was their goal—to be the best they could be. If that meant breaking the artificial barriers erected by society between the sexes, redefining what it meant to be a woman or facing ridicule day after day in their quest to achieve their goals, then that was exactly what they did.

Great Canadian Women: Nineteen Portraits of Extraordinary Women is about just this kind of woman. She wasn't out to prove anything. Her goal wasn't to show society what women were made of. She simply wanted to do what she knew, instinctively, she had to do.

Regardless the cost, these women lived their dreams and, in the process, provided the rest of us with examples of strength and fortitude to encourage us in our own journeys.

CHAPTER ONE

Anne Murray:
Canada's Songbird
(1945–)

Beneath this snowy mantle cold and clean,
The unborn grass lays waiting for its coat
to turn to green

–Gene MacLellan

Morna Anne Murray was born on June 20, 1945, in the small, maritime town of Springhill, Nova Scotia. Located about 45 kilometres from the New Brunswick border, the salty sea air of the Northumberland Strait to the northeast and the Bay of Fundy to the southwest had a way of seasoning its residents to the sometimes tumultuous life, which, during Anne's youth, was a predominantly coal-mining community. Springhill was no stranger to disaster, having witnessed the mine explosion of 1891 and a devastating underground fire in 1916. But by the time Anne was born in 1945, the community had yet to experience its most tragic history—the explosion in 1956 that claimed the lives of 39 miners and the 1958 Bump, which trapped 174 men. Seventy-five of those men never made it back to the surface alive. By the time these events occurred, Anne was old enough to understand their tragic implications.

Although the dictionary definition of Maritimer focuses on the geographical region this unique brand of Canadian calls home, it can't be ignored that to be a Maritimer means to be toughened by the harsh climate and the dangerous lifestyles associated with land and sea alike. It's a land that builds character in anyone who's willing to be assayed by fire.

Throughout her life and career, Anne Murray has shown her Maritime roots by her grit, fortitude and determination, hardworking attitude and steadfast belief in herself and her talent. The only daughter in a family with six children, it's not surprising that the bonny girl with the blonde mane preferred dungarees and athletics to frilly dresses and feminine frou-frou. But although Anne excelled in sports, it was her voice that captured Canada's collective heart.

As far back as I can remember, I sang. The first time I became aware that I could sing maybe a little better than others, I was driving in a car. I was nine years old, and I was singing along to the radio. My aunt-to-be was in the front seat and she turned to my mother and said, "My, Marion, she has a beautiful voice." I later found out that Aunt Kay was tone deaf, but I guess it doesn't mean she couldn't detect talent!

Singing was as important a staple in the Murray home as food and shelter. The family didn't need a special occasion to belt out a tune—every day was a singing day. By the age of 15, singing took on a new importance in Anne's life. For the next three years Anne travelled two hours by bus to Tatamagouche every Saturday morning for singing lessons.

While music was a lifelong passion, Anne had yet to embrace the possibility of a career in the industry and, planning for her future, attended the University of New Brunswick in Fredericton to study Physical Education.

It was her friends there who talked Anne into auditioning for *Singalong Jubilee*, a CBC TV show in 1964. When she didn't land a job at that first audition because the show already had enough altos on its cast, Anne was admittedly dejected. And when she was approached to audition a second time two years later by the show's co-host and associate producer, Bill Langstroth, she was initially reluctant. In the end, Bill's persistence paid off, and Anne accepted a contract to become a part of the 1966 cast of *Singalong Jubilee*. The terms of the contract were simple: "It is understood that you will be required to function either as a singer for a fee of seventy-one dollars and fifty cents ($71.50) per show or as a soloist for a fee of ninety-nine dollars ($99.00)." The fee was considerably more than the $25 a night she received singing at the Fredericton Curling Club. She debuted on the hit show on her 21st birthday.

Anne did graduate with a degree in Physical Education and blended a career as a teacher with her extracurricular singing. But after her first year in the classroom Anne knew she had to make a decision. With her summers dedicated to *Singalong Jubilee* and an offer to appear on the teen television show *Let's Go* during the regular season, Anne decided to give the music industry a try.

By the time Anne's hit single *Snowbird* catapulted the Canadian singer into the annals of our country's music history as being "the first time in history an American gold record was awarded to a solo Canadian female," she had recorded two albums. But it was *Snowbird*, written by Canadian songwriter Gene MacLellan and sung in Anne's warm, rich tones and perfect pitch, that propelled her into the hearts of music lovers everywhere.

Her sudden popularity throughout North America seemed to secure her place in the music industry. Anne's talents were in constant demand, with a steady stream of requests for her guest appearance on numerous television shows—a trend that over the years has included appearances on *The Bobby Vinton Show*, *Christmas with Friends of Sesame Street*, *Solid Gold*, *Saturday Night Live* and countless others.

But a life of stardom didn't change who Anne was as a person or a professional. She remained committed in her approach to her life and her music. Comfort was still king, and she frequently appeared on stage barefoot. In fact, her desire for comfort over fashion was highlighted in 1971 when she said she'd "never again play the International Hotel in Las Vegas. 'They want you to wear shoes, and they don't want you to wear hot pants because it'll hurt their image and, you know, the whole bit…That's not for me.'"

It took years before Anne came to understand that dressing for success on stage was almost as important as the talent she brought to her shows.

It's embarrassing to me now that I didn't know enough, but I just had no awareness about clothes. I never paid any attention to that kind of thing. I never thought it was important. I always thought that your personality and your talent were the most important things.

Although Anne was unwavering in her principles, she struggled with the rigours of her new life. She spent a considerable amount of time on airplanes, and for someone who hated to fly, she had to learn how to deal with that. Then there was the constant pressure to conform to the industry look, the push to fit her genre of music into a convenient box labelled "country," and the task of dealing with the overall adjustments that becoming an internationally renowned singer requires.

And despite the fact Anne was singing and producing more records, devising a follow-up hit to *Snowbird* was a challenge.

I was almost to the point of quitting…and yet I wasn't. There were just enough people around to encourage me. All I could think about was that I was a one-hit wonder. I figured that must be it because it had happened so many times before. I also knew I had the talent. The challenge was out there because I had a taste of it and I felt deep down it could be done.

By 1973, Capital Records put some extra money into the production of *Danny's Song*, and the resulting crossover pop-country hit proved that Anne had more than one hit single under her belt. With new management in play, the American market started showing some promise, and Anne was well on her way to reclaiming the recognition she had received just a few years before.

Meanwhile, her personal life was beginning to take a new direction. A relationship between Anne and her long-time friend and first manager, Bill Langstroth of *Singalong Jubilee* fame, was brewing.

In Barry Grills' book, *Snowbird: The Story of Anne Murray*, Bill is quoted as saying, "I thought she was singing to me right from the start. The voice went right through me and had me pinned like a specimen to the wall. Voompf!"

And despite the fact Bill was a married man 15 years her senior, the couple eventually married on June 20, 1975—Anne's 30th birthday.

While Anne has spent the majority of the last 30 years blending family and career, her priorities have never wavered. Nothing takes precedence over family and friends, and at all costs, ensuring some semblance of normalcy for her son William and daughter Dawn was always her first concern. Her success in the music world remains strong, with a top-10 hit as recently as 1990 and new albums being released regularly.

To date, Anne has received four Grammys, three American Music Awards, three Country Music Association Awards, three Canadian Country Music Association Awards and 31 Juno Awards. Anne was also honoured with the East Coast Music Association Directors' Special Achievement Award in 2001 and was inducted into the Juno Hall of Fame in 1993 and the Canadian Country Music Hall of Fame in 2002. She's a Companion of the Order of Canada—the highest honour that can be awarded to a Canadian civilian—and she was the first inductee into the Canadian Association of Broadcasters' Hall of Fame.

In addition, her name has been immortalized with a star on Hollywood and Vine, as well as on Canada's Walk of Fame in Toronto and in the Country Music Hall of Fame Walkway of Stars in Nashville. She's also received countless community accolades, such as being named an honourary lynx at the 25th anniversary celebration of the Lynx squadron at the Canadian Forces base in Chatham, New Brunswick, in 1973.

After almost four decades in the music business and 34 albums to her credit, her veins still flow with the salty sea air that characterizes towns and villages of Canada's Maritimes. A Maritimer through and through, Anne's stardom never coloured her vision of home. Her amazing talent not only raised the bar for Canadian singers, it put Canada on the map of the international music scene. She is truly Canada's songbird.

CHAPTER TWO

Mary Walsh:
Telling It Like It Is
(1952–)

I guess the theme of the honorary degrees could be Send in the Clowns. It seems fitting that yesterday the biggest clown in the country received his honorary degree. Prime Minister Jean Chretien, who has provided Canadians with so little in the way of what he had promised to provide and so much in the way of disappointed laughter. And so it is with some deep humility that I, having provided only a smidgen, a tiny, tiny, teeny portion of the laughs that Mr. Chretien has, that I stand here today with my esteemed colleagues…

–Mary Walsh during a convocation address at the Memorial University of Newfoundland, 2000

Whether she's the jack-of-all-trades Mamesanne Furey in the CBC television comedy *Hatching, Matching and Dispatching*, carrying on as the caustic Marg Delahunty in *This Hour Has 22 Minutes* or giving a speech at a university convocation, Mary Walsh is a tell-it-like-it-is kind'a gal.

Born in St. John's, Newfoundland, on May 13, 1952, Mary entered the world at a time when parents across North America were blaming the influence of the new wave of music known as rock and roll for encouraging rebellion in their children. But Mary's reasons for rebellion were quite different.

The seventh of eight children, Mary lived with her aunt and uncle after contracting pneumonia at the age of eight months. Initially, her move was said to be a precautionary one, but she never returned home. It was difficult for the sensitive youngster—living next door to her parents and all the while seeing how they seemingly had no problem accepting her seven other siblings. She never learned why she was handed over to her Aunt May. And it was a painful reality made even more difficult when her family moved to Conception Harbour after her father retired, leaving Mary behind.

The troubles in her family life led Mary to her first drink at the age of 13 and her rapid fall into alcoholism. But she's a survivor. She tackled her dependence on alcohol by joining Alcoholics Anonymous, overcame a failed teenage marriage and gradually dealt with the unresolved issues of her youth. Much later, when reflecting on the pain she'd felt at being "given away," Mary said, "That is the piece of sand that has made me the...pearl that I am today."

Living with her aunt and interacting with her troupe of lively, comical friends led Mary to develop her unique sense of humour. It's been said that laughter is the best medicine, and Mary's natural ability to cut straight to the point while seeing the humour in the mundane, the ordinary, even the tragic, helped Mary laugh at herself—and the world around her.

At the age of 18, Mary landed a summer job with CBC Radio as a radio announcer. Listeners must have liked what they heard because by the time the job ended, Mary was offered a part in a local play. From there she joined the Newfoundland Travelling Theatre Company (NTTC), where she met and "worked with Tommy Sexton, Greg Malone, Robert Joy, Dyan Olsen, Cathy Jones and Andy Jones, the future members of the CODCO troupe."

It was while Mary was studying drama at Ryerson Polytechnical Institute that she was approached again by the members of the NTTC to collaborate on another project—*Cod on a Stick*. Mary was involved in the writing of this performance, and it hit the stage at the Theatre Passe Muraille in Toronto. It was such a success that CBC brought the troupe back to St. John's to record the show for radio in 1974. The group also toured and developed other plays, and by 1988 a series of half-hour shows named *CODCO* hit the television screen. It was a resounding success and ran for five years.

Mary continued to do theatre work and movie productions simultaneously with her work on *CODCO*, and by the time that series ended, another was about to begin. *This Hour Has 22 Minutes* is a satirical take on weekly news, and for 11 years, Mary appeared in several roles. No subject is forbidden territory, and Mary, like her co-stars, uses black humour to tackle some tough topics.

In all her sketches, Mary blends in many of the characteristics she sees in the folk of her home base of Newfoundland—something she does with particular emphasis in a new pilot that aired on CBC television in early 2005 called *Hatching, Matching and Dispatching*. The show features a do-it-all family that operates a town business that effectively takes care of weddings, funerals and medical emergencies all from one home base. In Mary's point of view, her character, Mamesanne Furey, is someone you'd likely meet anywhere in Newfoundland.

"I feel that any one of those characters could walk right off the screen and into any community in Newfoundland [and] nobody would bat an eyelash," Mary said in a CBC interview, defending the show against some of its critics who thought it perpetuated stereotypes. "They are a real representation of some people. They're not representing all people...There are people just like the Fureys in Newfoundland."

What critics sometimes fail to recognize is that most Newfies know how to laugh at themselves—and others, for that matter. And Mary is determined to focus her career on humour—or at the very least, the humorous side of cynicism.

If *Hatching, Matching and Dispatching* moves from the pilot stage to that of a series on CBC, it won't make or break Mary's career. She's been hosting the CBC show *Open Book* since 2002 and continues her work in theatre, television and film.

Mary's been recognized with a host of Gemini Awards, was the recipient for best supporting actress at the Atlantic Film Festival in 1992, has received honorary degrees from two universities and was named a Member of the Order of Canada in 2000.

CHAPTER THREE

Louise Arbour:
Lady Justice
(1947–)

My daughter, my sister-in-law and I were not only raped. We were raped and beaten almost every day for a month. They put about 30 women and girls in a house. They beat up the other women so badly that they all died. Since the men doing this were people we knew, I suppose they spared my family so as to embarrass us.

–Maria Gorette, from an interview in "Rwanda: Death, Despair and Defiance," African Rights

BRITISH HISTORIAN LORD ACTON FIRST COINED THE SENTIMENT, "Every class is unfit to govern...Power tends to corrupt; absolute power corrupts absolutely." Acton, who died in 1902, had dedicated the majority of his life to the study of history, believing a sure way to mend the future is to study the past. Sadly, the world's political elite rarely takes advice from its academics, and since Acton's death, the world has witnessed more bloodshed resulting from war than it had in any century before.

It was a reality that Louise Arbour was protected from in the early part of her life. Born on February 10, 1947, to a middle-class Montréal family, Louise's early years were a struggle. Her parents may have tried to keep their small family together, but their stormy marriage eventually ended in divorce. Perhaps it was in an effort to protect Louise from the realities of her family situation that she was sent, at the age of 10, to College Regina Assumpta, an all-girls convent school.

The end result of this experience was that, by the time she graduated in 1967, Louise had had little contact with the outside world. Her reality was a classical education taught in French and a shared religious belief with those around her. It wasn't until she entered law school and couldn't buy her textbooks in French that she learned she was a member of an ethnic minority at that time in Canada.

Attending law school during the Front de Liberation du Québec (FLQ) crisis was likely one of Louise's first experiences with political upheaval. It also served to define the kind of lawyer, and the kind of judge, Louise would eventually become. While on the one hand Louise was disturbed by the federal government's use of the War Measures Act, seeing it as a violation of human rights, she did understand the motivation behind the action. The discovery of Québec Justice Minister Pierre Laport's dead body in the trunk of a car was a prime example of the upheaval of the day. It was precisely Louise's unique ability to remain objective and not colour her decisions with personal biases that drew the attention of Richard Goldstone, a South African judge.

Goldstone was "on loan to the United Nations from the newly constituted South African Constitutional Court for a two-year period" and had been appointed the Chief United Nations (UN) Prosecutor in Yugoslavia and Rwanda in August 1994. He'd first met Louise in 1990 when the two attended a legal conference at Witwatersrand University in Cape Town, and they became fast friends. They met again at another conference a year later.

Nearing the end of his two-year term for the UN, Goldstone was anxious to return to his previous way of life. He recognized early on in his tenure that he wasn't cut out for the bureaucracy rampant in large organizations like the UN, but he was still concerned for the cause of the International War Crimes Tribunals (IWCT) in both Yugoslavia and Rwanda. And he believed Louise would be the perfect successor to the job. Not only did he admire her professionalism and bilingualism, but she was also a woman—a quality he thought especially important when dealing with the cases of rape being brought forward by investigators.

At that point in her career, Louise's name was often in the midst of controversy in Canada. In

1987 she served as vice-president of the Canadian Civil Liberties Association and argued for the overturning of the rape shield law. After a 10-year battle by Canadian feminists, a law was established to prohibit questions of past sexual history directed toward alleged victims of rape during cross-examination. Louise argued it was unconstitutional, and although she wasn't the sole decision-maker in the case, she was the lone woman on the team. She bore the brunt of criticism from feminist groups, but she stood her ground, arguing there was "nothing to gain in protecting women if innocent men are convicted...it will take only one wrongful conviction for all the gains that women have made in this area to be lost."

In 1990 Louise accepted an appointment to the Ontario Supreme Court and two years later was part of a panel arguing for a prisoner's right to vote. But perhaps the most controversial decision of her career was her part in a three-person decision to acquit Imre Finta of war crimes. The Hungarian-born Canadian was accused of committing war crimes against Jews in World War II. Louise argued that "by definition [Nazi war crimes] do not meet stringent domestic evidence rules." The decision sent the Canadian Jewish community into turmoil, and Louise was thought of as "making Canada a safe place for Nazis."

When Goldstone approached Louise with his plan to put her name forward as his possible

successor, Louise was in the midst of an inquiry
into the Prison for Women in Kingston where
women prisoners were said to have endured
"cruel, inhuman and degrading treatment" at the
hands of a male riot squad. But despite her
involvement in relatively high-profile cases, few in
the legal community outside of Canada had heard
of her. And because of her controversial decisions,
her approval rating in Canada was something to be
desired.

UN Secretary-General Boutros Boutros-Ghali
wasn't deterred by reports that Louise wasn't a
friend of women and, after her decision in the
Imre Finta affair, that she "couldn't be trusted to
prosecute war crimes from any era, anywhere."
But Louise would have to win over the members
of the Security Council and, in particular, its
chair—one very powerful woman by the name of
Madeleine Albright, U.S. Ambassador to the UN.

The two women met over coffee arranged by
Robert Fowler, Canadian Ambassador to the UN.
Albright brought an entourage of a half-dozen officials from the U.S. State Department to examine
Louise, but the two women first had a tête-à-tête.
They were two strong women with many similar-
ities, and they immediately liked each other. By
the end of Louise's meeting with Albright, and
then the other officials, Louise more than made up
for her poor press. She received her appointment
on February 29, 1996, and by that fall she was

heavily researching the histories and touring both countries under her charge.

She visited the mass gravesite in Vukovar, Croatia, while it was under exhumation. It was the site of a slaughter where Serbian soldiers rounded up non-Serbs in the town of Vukovar on November 20, 1991. When they could not find the men they were looking for, the soldiers proceeded to the hospital in town. The men had taken refuge there, thinking they'd be safe, but the Serbian soldiers took them and others—a total of 280 people—out of their hospital beds, crutches and canes and bandages and all, and led them to a farm just out of town.

The Serbs forced hospital patients to walk out into a field with the men who had tried to hide among them. They were beaten, some with their own crutches, then killed. Many bodies, still in their pyjamas, were found tangled together (some of them fused in an embrace, indicating they hadn't died instantly), some with bandages, broken crutches and, in one case, catheter tube still attached.

To say that scenes like these and the stories behind them were shocking is an understatement. But it wasn't until Louise began delving into the process of arresting those indicted for war crimes that she realized just how difficult her job was going to be. The UN policy was that the "indicted people were to be arrested by the countries that hosted them." She approached the North Atlantic

Treaty Organisation (NATO), seeking their help in arresting the criminals, but all she received was reassurance that this would happen when peace was secured. Frustrated, but not deterred, Louise decided she had to play the hand she was dealt and tackled the problems over the next four years like moves in an enormously complex game of strategy.

Whereas before her tenure indictments were made public, and the people under suspicion were always on guard, Louise began making "secret indictments." Slavko Dokmanovic, the Serbian president of the municipality of Vukovar who was involved in the massacre there, was among the first to be indicted this way. He didn't know he'd been indicted on crimes against humanity until he was called to check on one of his properties, and UN soldiers captured him.

If Louise thought the situation in Yugoslavia was challenging, the IWCT there was like a well-oiled machine compared to its counterpart in Rwanda. Before she could even start her job, she had to deal with workers who didn't have pencils, paper or telephones, much less computers. Apparently, an unscrupulous registrar misspent the meagre budget the IWCT had to work with in that country. Louise confronted the UN legal office in New York with her information. An audit was ordered, and several people lost their jobs—including the registrar. While still far from a perfect working environment, Louise could now finally get to work.

After lengthy negotiations, Louise managed to convince Kenyan President Daniel Arap Moi to allow representatives of the UN to infiltrate his country and capture Hutu officials who had fled there from Rwanda. It was a tough sell, but Louise convinced Moi that the move would earn him foreign support and, after all, there was an election coming up. The subsequent raid landed them seven Hutu elite, and even though it was discovered that one of the seven was captured as the result of mistaken identity, she retained the respect she'd earned.

But Louise's biggest accomplishment was yet to come. Before she left her position as chief prosecutor for the UN, she indicted the Yugoslav president himself, Slobodan Milosevic, on charges of war crimes. Milosevic made his debut in Serbian politics in 1987 and by 1989 was elected President of Serbia. In 1997 he became president of what was then the Yugoslav Federation. Throughout his career he was considered somewhat of a loose cannon, but his hunger for absolute power was his downfall. On May 22, 1999, Milosevic was indicted for "crimes against humanity and violations of the customs of war," following his involvement with attacks on the Albanian population of Kosovo on January 15 of the same year.

It was the first time a leader of a state had ever been indicted for this crime while still in power. While Louise was responsible for the situation, she never heard his case. She left her position as the chief prosecutor for the IWCT in 1999 for an appointment with the Supreme Court of Canada. She had fought the good fight for four years, and it was time to return to her home country. In 2004 Louise was appointed as the UN High Commissioner for Human Rights.

Perhaps Louise's one regret was her inability to establish long-term sexual assault committees in Rwanda and Yugoslavia. It was difficult to prove rape, aside from personal testimony. And women who came forward with such allegations were frequently ostracized, ridiculed, or worse, and because no witness protection program was in place, many victims simply chose not to testify. Louise was quoted as saying in one interview, "I think part of the difficulty is that up to this point, we have not been able to substantiate [stories of rape] with the kind of evidence you need to prove a criminal case." With the horrible stories some survivors shared, it must have been a great burden for her to recognize her limitations. Still, she focused on what she was able to achieve—and it was considerably more than many would have thought possible.

CHAPTER FOUR

Marion Alice (Powell) Orr:
With Eyes to the Skies
(1918–1995)

*Within all of us is a varying amount of space lint
and stardust, the residue from our creation.
Most are too busy to notice it, and it is stronger
in some than others. It is strongest in those of us
who fly and is responsible for an unconscious,
subtle desire to slip into some wings and try for
the elusive boundaries of our origin.*

–K.O. Eckland, *Footprints on Clouds*

IT TAKES A UNIQUE TYPE OF INDIVIDUAL TO BECOME AN
airplane pilot. The person needs a mathematical
mind that can absorb all the information displayed
in the cockpit and make sense of it. The capacity to
make quick decisions in a fraction of a second is
also a must. And the ability to put into perspective
life and death—the knowledge that as you soar
through the air you are precariously positioned in
exactly such a spot.

Marion Alice Orr was just that sort of individual.

On June 25, 1918, in Toronto, Ontario, Marion came into the world with great excitement and just the right amount of space lint and stardust to bode her well as she grew into a modern, 20th-century woman. Bucking the trend that nice young ladies worked through their school years primarily in preparation to become wives and mothers, Marion had her eyes fixed firmly skyward.

At the age of 15, with nothing more than a Grade 8 education, Marion packed her bags and headed out into the world with one goal—the dream of taking flying lessons and earning a pilot's licence. To accomplish her goal, she took a job at a factory, and of the $10 a week she earned in wages, $6 went to pay for an hour of flying lessons. She willingly went without food if it meant another hour in the air.

She had her first lesson on April 22, 1939, and by June 9 of the same year, she took her first solo flight. Six months later, on January 5, 1940, she earned her private pilot's licence, and by December 1941, she earned her commercial pilot's licence. Shortly thereafter, she met and married one of her instructors, D.K. "Deke" Orr, and together the couple worked on Marion earning her instructor's rating, which she succeeded in doing on September 25, 1942.

One of these milestones alone was a huge accomplishment. Collectively, however, Marion had done what few women in the world had done at that time. And although it seemed unlikely that a woman could get a job flying a plane in the 1940s, she again broke the trend when, on October 2, 1942, "Marion was hired to be the manager and chief flight instructor at St. Catharines Flying Club. She was the first woman in Canada to operate a flying club."

But her career in St. Catharines was cut short after a fire destroyed five aircraft, and the school was closed. World War II was also absorbing most of the effort when it came to flight training. As a result, Marion was forced to find employment as a control tower operator, and again was only the second woman to be hired in this kind of position and then, only on a trial basis. Marion continued to look for opportunities to fly and even contacted the Royal Canadian Air Force (RCAF). They turned her down. No matter how ardently she could defend her abilities, no woman had ever flown in the RCAF. Unfairly grounded, Marion felt dejected.

While stories of how Marion first heard of the Air Transport Auxiliary (ATA) differ depending on the source, it's clear that she was one of five Canadian women who were awarded jobs with the British organization. That itself was a feat because, like the RCAF, the ATA didn't look favourably on women pilots. In a commentary by C.G. Grey, editor of the publication *Aeroplan*, it's obvious that this sentiment was deeply felt:

We quite agree…there are millions of women in the country who could do useful jobs in war. But the trouble is that so many of them insist on wanting to do jobs which they are quite incapable of doing. The menace is the woman who thinks that she ought to be flying in a high-speed bomber when she really has not the intelligence to scrub the floor of a hospital properly or who wants to nose around as an Air Raid Warden and yet can't cook her husband's dinner.

The commentary went on to compare these inadequate women to men who didn't like taking orders and had an overabundance of self-confidence for the amount of their experience—one of the main causes of crashes "in aeroplanes and other ways." Life is full of ironies, and though Grey may have thought his argument well presented and sound, it received a lot of opposition from men and women alike.

Pauline Gower was said to have rallied against this sentiment perhaps the most forcefully. A commercial pilot with more than 2000 hours in the air and a position as a commissioner in the Civil Air Guard, it was through Pauline's tireless efforts that women were accepted into the ATA as pilots of smaller aircraft, such as the Tiger Moth. And on January 1, 1940, the first eight of the eventual 166 women to join the 1300 men in service at the ATA took to the skies. "This was the first time in history (in England, or anywhere else in the world) that women would be officially employed in ferrying military aircraft."

As these women displayed their competence in the air, they received the qualifications necessary to pilot larger, more challenging aircraft. Of the 166 women serving in the ATA shuttling planes "between factories, storage depots and squadrons" until the end of the war, five were Canadian. Marion Orr was among them.

"I was there to fly and I just loved it…I wish I could go back," Marion said in the CBC documentary *Spitfires in the Rhododendrons*, which aired on June 3, 1994. "There was something about the Spitfire—you really thought you had something there."

By the end of the war, women were flying almost all manner of aircraft, including Hurricanes, Mosquitoes and Spitfires—the latter often referred to as a lady's airplane because of its sleek lines and small, light build.

"It was a continual challenge to fly so many different types (of aircraft)…But an airplane is an airplane; maybe different speeds, different knobs, heavier, but that didn't bother me."

The end of the war didn't mark the end of Marion's flying career. Although jobs in the field were still scarce for women, Marion mixed civilian instruction with training as an aero mechanic, and by 1950 she purchased Aero Activities Ltd. She became the first Canadian woman to "own and operate a flying club." In 1954 she moved her school and reopened it a year later, amid much opposition, as Maple Airport in Maple, Ontario.

Not one to let the grass grow under her feet, Marion continued to conquer other goals and challenges, becoming the first woman in Canada to obtain a helicopter licence on May 16, 1960. It was while in a helicopter with one of her students that she experienced engine failure and was involved in a serious accident. Her student wasn't injured, but Marion broke her back and was hospitalized for several months before returning to the skies. But return she did, and after many months of recuperation in Florida, Marion returned to Canada to teach.

Although she loved to fly, it was hard on her injured back, and in 1963 Marion took a hiatus from flying until 1975. She then recertified and returned to teaching, this time for Toronto Airways Ltd. By 1981 Marion had "an instructor's rating, Class 1 with instrument endorsement, multi-engine, single engine land and sea and was a Designated Flight Test Examiner."

She continued to teach until 1985 when she retired for a grand total of two weeks before deciding retirement really wasn't for her. She returned to teaching on a freelance basis until poor health forced her to turn in her licence in 1994. By that time she had clocked 20,000 hours in the air and had taught upwards of 5000 student pilots.

Marion was recognized for her achievements many times. She was a member of the Canadian Ninety-Nines—a group of women pilots that first formed in 1929. The group, initially formed as a support network for the 117 licensed American women pilots, "organize air safety seminars and courses, they are active in civilian air search and rescue training, winter survival training and sponsoring Transport Canada enrichment courses."

In 1976 Marion was awarded the Amelia Earhart Medallion by the First Canadian Chapter, Ninety-Nines. She was inducted into the Canadian Aviation Hall of Fame in 1982 and into the Ninety-Nines Forest of Friendship in Kansas in 1989, and she received the Order of Canada in 1993.

While the fear of flying is a common phobia, the skies never betrayed Marion. She died in 1995 in Peterborough, Ontario, in an automobile accident. The little girl with space lint and stardust in her eyes not only accomplished her goal of becoming a pilot, she lived her dream for most of her 77 years.

CHAPTER FIVE

Silken Laumann:
It's All About Focus
(1964–)

The rhythmic sound of the oars dipping into the crystal-clear lake was soothing, ever so slightly easing the pain reverberating through her injured leg. As she rowed steadily, back and forth, back and forth and back again, she refused to let the pain overwhelm her. Just a few weeks before, while warming up for the pre-Olympic trials in Essen, Germany, her shell had been hit by another shell carrying a German pairs team. Her shell was sliced through by the force, and more than 200 pieces of wood had embedded themselves in her lower leg. Her muscles were ripped and torn, bones broken. The pain only eased slightly by the shock of it all. Still, she didn't let herself be overcome by imaginings. Focus. Focus on the task at hand. Get help. Figure out the rest later. And now, here she was again, just 27 days and five operations after the accident, and she was rowing. She couldn't even walk yet, but she would row. And she would compete. And in the end, she would win an Olympic medal.

SILKEN LAUMANN DIDN'T NECESSARILY SET OUT TO BE AN Olympic rower, but ever since she was first captivated by the gymnastic prowess of Romania's Nadia Comaneci, she knew she wanted to do something that magnificent. Born in 1964 in Mississauga, Ontario, Silken was about the same age as the perfect-10 gymnast. It was Nadia's strength, perseverance and obvious ability to concentrate on the task at hand that captivated Silken, and she was mesmerized by it all.

Silken was tall for her age, and gymnastics wasn't likely the best fit for a girl who'd grow to be five-feet and 10-inches. On the other hand, track seemed like a good place to start. It was a natural choice for the youngster who loved cycling through the neighbourhood, playing tag, capture the flag and just about any other run-and-fetch game you could think of. Silken had energy to burn and was naturally active, so organizing that energy into a competition wasn't a huge leap.

But it wasn't until her older sister Daniele coaxed her to try rowing that Silken had found her home. In 1984, at the age of 19, she and Daniele, a member of the National Rowing Team, won a bronze medal at the Olympics in Los Angeles. By then she'd already proven herself on the world stage, having won "a gold medal in quadruple sculls at the U.S. Championships and a gold medal in single sculls at the Pan American Games."

Even though she was a natural behind the oars, Silken struggled with back problems. She'd been diagnosed with a pinched sciatic nerve—a painful condition that causes mild to severe throbbing in the back and legs. At its worst, someone with this condition shouldn't bend, lift, or strain their body in any way. Yet with the help of physiotherapy and a rigid training schedule, Silken continued to row.

Her hard work paid off. In 1987 she won a second gold medal at the Pan American Games in Indianapolis, and in 1990 she earned the silver medal at the World Championships in Lake Barrington, Australia.

In 1990 Silken moved from Mississauga, Ontario, to Victoria, BC, where she began training year-round with coach Mike Spracklen, and the next year, in Vienna, Austria, she won the World Championship in single sculls.

By this time, Silken was known for her consistently strong performance in competition, her ability to persevere through often difficult and painful physical problems and her overall excellence as an athlete. But it wasn't until May 1992, just a few months before the summer Olympics in Barcelona, when a tragic accident between her racing shell and that of a German pairs team nearly ended her athletic career, that the world would see just how determined and how persistent an athlete she really was.

It took five operations over a period of 10 days, as well as a skin graft, to repair the damage from that accident. Doctors warned Silken she might not be able to row recreationally again, never mind compete. But three weeks after the accident she had her husband, Olympian John Wallace, carry her from her wheelchair to her shell. She had just five weeks to recuperate and bring herself up to competitive standards. Against all odds, she stunned the world by earning a bronze medal that same year.

Silken went on to win other competitions—and she overcame other disappointments. In 1995, after testing positive for a banned substance at the Pan American Games in Argentina, Silken and her three teammates were stripped of their gold medal. The banned substance, the world would later discover, was pseudoephedrine, a decongestant in the Benadryl Allergy and Decongestant medication she'd taken for a cold. It was a devastating blow, especially since a doctor had given her the green light to take Benadryl. The doctor hadn't explained that while some Benadryl products were okay to take, the ones containing pseudoephedrine were not because that ingredient can act as a stimulant. (Ironically, in 2004 pseudoephedrine was removed from the list of banned substances because it is not a performance-enhancing drug.)

For Silken, losing the gold medal for herself and her teammates was overwhelming, as was the damage to her reputation. And though it was a worry, it was another challenge she'd face head-on and, eventually, overcome. Later that same year she was awarded the Canadian Olympic Order, and she earned a silver medal in the single sculls at the 1996 Olympic Games in Atlanta, Georgia.

Along with her athletic achievements, Silken has been awarded numerous accolades, including the 1997 Wilma Rudolph Courage Award; an Honorary Doctorate of Laws from the University of Victoria, McMaster University and the University of Windsor; and the 1999 Thomas Keller Medal. She was also inducted into the Canadian Sports Hall of Fame in 1998. But if you asked her today what her greatest accomplishment is, she'd likely point to her two children—William and Kate.

In March 1999 Silken retired from her professional athletic career to refocus her energies on her family, as well as on her freelance writing and inspirational speaking. And she has recently combined her love of children with her passion for sport and formed The Silken Laumann Active Kids Movement, an organization dedicated to increasing physical activity in Canadian children.

Her goal is to "help our kids harness the power of play," to inspire youngsters, their families, their schools and communities to create opportunities for children to gather together and play as a way to increase healthy living, tackle boredom among youth and, in some cases, even reduce teen violence. Hoops Unlimited is an example of the latter. In 2002 a group of Etobicoke churches opened the doors to their churches and encouraged youth to play basketball and other sports. "Once the kids were hooked on hoops, the churches brought in motivational speakers who spoke about life choices and personal potential."

For Silken, every day brings with it a new and wonderful challenge—one she'll meet with the same persistence and focus she's met every other challenge that's come her way.

CHAPTER SIX

Flora MacDonald:
So Much To Do
(1926–)

Night falls early in the winter months in North Sydney, Nova Scotia. Too early for some youngsters still interested in play and with energy to spend. Not so for the MacDonald clan. Supper has been put away, and the evening chores done. So there was no baseball to look forward to on a long, cold winter's night. This evening would wend its way through calamity, mystery and daring adventures only limited by human imagination. What tonight's story would be, they weren't sure. But Papa MacDonald wouldn't disappoint his young daughters. They huddled together at his feet, snug in blankets handmade for each of them—blankets just like the one their mother was working on that very moment as she, too, listened in. And together, the family embarked on a new journey. As Papa MacDonald opened the book, the girls could hear the spine crack. A good sign—this would be a story they'd never heard before. And when he started reading with that gentle, patient voice of his, the girls were not disappointed. "Call me Ishmael," he began…

TO SAY FLORA MACDONALD WAS BORN INTO POLITICS wouldn't be a stretch. Her father, perhaps the biggest motivation in her life's journey, took her to her first political meeting when she was 10, and she was thrilled at the prospect. Flora's extracurricular activities extended to after-school sport and church events, so the thought of sitting in on a meeting of men discussing issues she'd never heard of stirred her imaginings just as her father's nightly readings did. What was public policy? Fiscal irresponsibility? Tariff tinkering? She would bombard her father with these and so many other questions following that first sojourn into the world of politics.

Flora made her grand entry into the world on June 3, 1926. Parents Frederick and Molly MacDonald were thrilled—theirs was a home where there was always room for one more. Flora was the third child born to the MacDonald clan of North Sydney, Nova Scotia, but there'd be more to come, each one as eagerly anticipated as the one before.

The inquisitive mind that characterizes Flora's life was something her parents encouraged in all their children. Her father subscribed to five different newspapers, read current events to his family and inspired debate. While theirs wasn't a life of material affluence, it was rich in experience and in love. With a steadfast, Christian mother and a hard-working, eclectic father, the MacDonald children received all the right tools to become the best people they could be.

From an early age, Flora was well-known for her energy and enthusiasm for life and for the occasional time when that spunk would get her into trouble—like the time a stone just happened to make its way from her hand through the Reverend John S. Sutherland's living room window, knocking down a full bottle of milk in the process. She apologized, of course, and while the accident may have made her a little more careful, it didn't dull her exuberance.

It was a natural tendency that covered all aspects of her life, including her school and church education. She refused to learn things half way, wanting every question that occurred to her answered before she was ready to move on to the next lesson. Such was the case with her Catechism classes, which she attended at the age of 12. Her family's church provided what they called "Shortened Catechism." While the minister encouraged his students to memorize questions and responses, Flora wanted a more thorough understanding. The situation eventually came to a head when her father told her to do the memorization requested, or memorize an equivalent portion of the Bible. She chose the Bible over her Catechism.

Flora's desire to understand everything to its fullest was dimmed, somewhat, when she was directed to business college after her graduation from high school. She desperately wanted to attend university, but the money to do so simply wasn't in the family budget.

This was the one time when I really questioned my father's direction in my life. I wanted to go on to university, but in Cape Breton at the time it was just not feasible, except for the daughters of well-to-do people…While I wanted to go the university route, and inwardly felt that if my dad had really wanted me to go he could have found some way to get there, I was told it wasn't possible. I accepted it, although with a heavy heart, and decided to go to Business College.

Although business college wasn't where Flora ultimately wanted to be, she discovered years down the road how that education, and her subsequent work experience, helped carve her into a political force to be reckoned with. Her first job, as a junior clerk at the Bank of Nova Scotia, earned her $40 a month. It was a job she held for six years, climbing her way up the corporate ladder to ledger keeper, teller and then assistant accountant. It was there that Flora first experienced the discrepancies between advancement and its pay raise and an employee's gender. She noted that a female colleague of hers had responsibilities that didn't match the woman's title, or her wage. Despite the fact that women had won the right to vote and sit in the Senate, in the 1940s, the world still didn't treat men and women as equals in the workplace. It just didn't make sense to her that an employee doing quality work would be positioned and paid less because she was a woman. The situation infuriated Flora.

At that point in her life, Flora could do little to change the situation. Eventually, she transferred to the bank's head office in Toronto and continued to work and save money until she earned enough to take a holiday. It would be the first of many trips across the Atlantic, the Pacific and all places in-between.

Her first trip of significance occurred in July 1952 when Flora and her mother travelled to England. For her mother, the trip was a wonderful opportunity to connect with distant relatives. For Flora, it was a chance to really spread her wings, delve into her family history and learn all she could about the world. She hitchhiked her way throughout the British Isles, even managing a stop at the gravesite of her namesake—Flora MacDonald, the Highland heroine who helped Prince Charles Edward Stuart escape Scotland after "leading an unsuccessful rebellion against English domination."

It was an education she'd cherish for all time and one she would repeat. But for now, she had her mind set on getting a job in London, England. A year later she and a friend traversed the countryside again, this time on an eight-week excursion Flora dubbed "Our Great Continental Tour" before heading back to Canada.

For the next few years Flora took a job to earn enough money to finance another trip, visit another destination and then do it all over again. After all, she was a young woman in her 20s with her whole future ahead of her and more than enough time to settle down. The world was an open book full of exciting adventures, and she couldn't stop for long before leaping into the next chapter.

Her interest in the world of politics is something Flora took with her on her travels. Having been schooled from an early age on the importance of being well read and informed of current events, Flora kept up with the news of the day and even visited the British Parliament when it was in session.

Back in Canada, Flora assisted with the odd election campaign until one day, after having recently moved to Ottawa in 1957, she happened across the Progressive Conservative Association of Canada's main headquarters. She stopped in and asked to have her name moved to a voting list in the riding where she now lived. On a lark, she asked if any clerical positions were open. Initially, she was told no. But when Flora pressed, mentioning her work in the most recent provincial election in Nova Scotia, she was introduced to the executive secretary and given a job on a temporary, weekly basis. The pay was $60 a week—a good salary in those days.

But the opportunity to work for the Progressive Conservatives (PCs), a party with views and ideals she held close to her heart, meant more than the weekly paycheque. In a letter home, Flora shared her excitement with her parents: "Don't say I didn't warn you before I left home of the type of work I would be doing when I reached Ottawa. You can see by the letterhead that I've really and truly joined the party…"

The country was gearing up for a federal election, and Flora found herself moving from one office to another, assisting wherever she was needed. John Diefenbaker was leader of the PCs at that time, and Flora witnessed the party's election and Diefenbaker's rise to the position of prime minister. It was the first election since 1930 that saw a conservative victory, and the party was energized by the result.

Flora had proven herself such an asset in the four weeks since her arrival that she went from being an extra pair of hands in the office to secretary for the prime minister's chief adviser. She remained at PC headquarters for the next nine years, witnessing exciting times and, unfortunately, the disappointments that often accompany them.

Such was the case with Diefenbaker himself. An ardent supporter of the charismatic leader at the beginning of his career, Flora watched the party's popularity swell and capture 208 seats in the 1958 election. She also witnessed its support plummet, losing 92 of those seats in the 1962 election. While

Diefenbaker led his government to a third, consecutive win, it was by a narrow margin indeed. Flora remained faithful, even after a severe rift in the party pitted Diefenbaker against as many as 10 of his own cabinet ministers.

Diefenbaker's minority government fought for survival when another election was held in 1963. The PCs lost that election, as well as another two years later. Eventually, being the reasonable person she was, Flora, too, became concerned that the party's leader was losing his grip. She realized she'd have to choose between supporting a leader who was fast becoming a liability, or the party whose values and beliefs she held dear. Apparently, Flora must have been seen talking to the wrong people because after nine years of dedicated service, Flora was fired under suspicion of being disloyal.

To say the experience was heart wrenching is an understatement. Flora had given all she had and more to a job that meant everything to her. She reeled from disappointment for a time, but it wasn't long before she landed a job in the political studies department at Queen's University. Years later, Professor Hugh Thorburn of Queen's political studies department said:

Flora's dismissal threw her out of the party organization and therefore made her a freewheeling individual who wasn't an employee anymore. But she was still a Tory and very highly regarded…If she had continued as

*a party bureaucrat she would simply have been a knowl-
edgeable person behind the scenes, without great personal significance. Her dismissal turned into a public
figure a person who would not otherwise have been one.
The incident made her available for high office.*

The following year she campaigned vigorously
for Robert Stanfield's leadership bid of the federal
PC party. She'd supported his bid as premier of
Nova Scotia in 1956 and again in 1960, and he
hadn't disappointed. She knew he'd shine in the
position of party leader and, eventually, prime
minister.

Meanwhile, Flora continued working at Queen's
and campaigned for and won the position of
national secretary. Along with juggling these two
responsibilities, Flora took on the role of president
of the Elizabeth Fry Society and immediately
began working toward the development of a
halfway house for women in a pre-release program. It was a cause dear to her heart, not only
because it involved the social issue of the reinte-
gration of incarcerated women into society, but
also because she believed in community service.

By 1970 Flora took on another challenge—that
of directorship of the Committee for an Independent Canada. And in 1971 she made history as the
first woman to be accepted into Canada's National
Defense College. It was another step towards her
eventual foray into politics as the first woman to
run for election in the riding of Kingston in 1972.

When the time came, Flora's campaign spin-doctors developed the slogan "Be In Touch." Those three small words said so much about Flora's commitment to society, to community and to the person who went to the ballot box to vote. She cared about people—for Flora, the people were the only reason to be in politics. And each emotion-packed statement quoted and published in one newspaper or another only endeared her to her electorate even more than the one before.

Flora's criticism of the ruling Liberal government was quoted at length in one newspaper, calling it a "massive failure of democratic leadership" and charging that "the government had its chance to pull Canada together...but it failed the challenge and dashed our hopes...Ottawa's technocrats have no feeling for the lives they are playing with so casually."

Flora triumphed over her opponents in the Kingston riding where she ran, and her first session in parliament was in the position of Conservative critic of Indian and Northern Affairs. Like any other challenge that came her way, Flora delved into her new portfolio with vigour. In keeping with her motto, "Be In Touch," Flora arranged visits to all the Native bands. At the same time she didn't limit her concerns, or her influence in the House, to her portfolio. She used question period to challenge the leading party on issues involving everything from immigration and high school dropouts to capital punishment and amendments to the British North American Act. It wasn't long before the new girl in town proved herself to be informed, intelligent and more than capable of taking any criticism thrown at her.

Flora's first term as a Member of Parliament (MP) was a short one. The Liberal government fell in 1974 over a motion on the new budget. It was back to the polls, and despite the fact that Flora had endeared herself to her constituents, she was concerned with the timing of this election. She was right to be worried. Despite their fall, the Liberals walked away as victors in 1974, capturing a majority with 140 seats to the Tories 95.

"Flora MacDonald had polled 17,795 votes in her riding. She was the only PC woman candidate who made it." For the next four years Flora served as the critic of Housing and Urban Affairs. And as before, she continued to voice her concerns over key issues of the day: women in politics, Canadian nationalism, economic growth, inflation, Canada's resource policy and more.

Her efforts didn't go unnoticed. When Robert Stanfield announced his resignation as party leader prior, in 1975, Flora was a natural candidate for the position. And she didn't jump into the leadership race without doing a lot of research on her chances at a win and receiving considerable support. When her name was officially put forward as a candidate by the Mayor of Toronto, David Crombie, she was the lone woman in a list of

11 leadership hopefuls that included Joe Clark and Brian Mulroney.

Although expected as a leading contender in the race, Flora placed sixth after the first ballot with 214 votes—less than 10 percent of the votes cast. It was a shocking blow. After coming in fifth in the second ballot, Flora decided to throw her support behind Joe Clark, and she bowed out of the race. Clark eventually won the leadership race by 65 votes, pulling ahead of Claude Wagner who'd been in the lead until the final ballot.

When critics poured over the results, honing in on Flora's poor showing, the only answer was a painfully distressing one—she was a woman.

Robert Jamieson of *The Financial Post* wrote, "The idea that Canada may not be ready for a woman prime minister—which is what the exercise is all about—still has too much life in it."

Flora remained MP for Kingston and the Islands until November 1988. During that time, she held three cabinet posts under Prime Minister Brian Mulroney: "Secretary of State for External Affairs, the first woman in Canada to be named to the prestigious Foreign Minister portfolio; Minister of Employment and Immigration; and Minister of Communications and Culture."

Since losing her seat in 1988, Flora has worked on the boards of numerous organizations, including the International Development Research Centre,

Partnership Africa Canada, the Canadian Council for Refugees, Commonwealth Human Rights Initiative and the Carnegie Commission on the Prevention of Deadly Conflict. She's earned countless accolades, including the Order of Canada, Companion of the Order of Canada, Order of Ontario and the Pearson Peace Medal.

In August 2004, Flora was honoured for her social development work in India by being the first Canadian ever to receive a Padamshree—a special medal of honour awarded by the Indian government in recognition of exceptional service. Her focus there includes "combating infant mortality, promoting literacy training, conserving forests and setting up income generation schemes in Arunachal Pradesh and Uttranchal."

While Flora may have hung up her political ambitions in Canada, her main focus today is on development issues in developing countries.

Now in her "golden years," Flora shows no signs of slowing down and enjoying retirement. Why bother? Life is far too exciting, and there's still so much to learn and do.

CHAPTER SEVEN

The Famous Five:
Emily Murphy, Nellie McClung, Henrietta Muir Edwards, Louise McKinney, Irene Parlby

I believe that never was a country better adapted to produce a great race of women than this Canada of ours, nor a race of women better adapted to make a great country.

–Emily Murphy

BORN TO THE WEALTHY FERGUSSON FAMILY ON MARCH 14, 1868, in Cookstown, Ontario, Emily Murphy never had to worry about the necessities of life. Nor, for that matter, did she ever consider herself anything less than an equal to her brothers—a sentiment shared by her father. So it's no wonder that as the wife of an Anglican priest, Emily Murphy exuded confidence and was well suited to public life. She was a model minister's wife, tending to all her family's needs and keeping active in the church and the community in which they lived. She had a keen mind, keeping well informed of the issues of the day. She also had a kind heart for the less fortunate in society.

As the Murphys moved from place to place, Emily lent a hand wherever she saw a need or felt a calling. By that point Emily had already garnered considerable success as the fiction writer Janey Canuck, writing her first novel under that name in 1898. She was active in several organizations and was the president of the Canadian Women's Press Club for a time. By the time the family settled in Edmonton, Alberta, Emily's volunteer resume was considerable indeed, and she'd have to call on all the knowledge and experience she'd accumulated throughout the years to make her biggest contribution to Canadian society yet.

It was during one happenstance interaction between Emily and one farmer's wife that she learned Canadian women had no protection under the law. The woman said that her husband had sold the farm, but hadn't bothered to tell her, and he was legally within his rights not to do so. "There were no property laws on the books that protected a wife's interest in the family home or even gave her the right to know of transactions involving her home."

It was absurd, to Emily's mind, and she was definitely going to do something about it. Researching laws at the legislative building's library and discussing the issue with Henrietta Muir Edwards— the convener of laws for the National Council of Women (NCW)—Emily determined that there was a desperate need for a Dower Act that would "protect women in the disposition of family property."

In her quest for this kind of legislation, Emily petitioned the Alberta government, and in 1910, R.B. Bennett, a Member of the Legislative Assembly (MLA) for Calgary at the time, introduced the bill to the legislature. Despite Emily's best efforts, it was defeated. But she didn't give up, and in 1911 the Married Women's Protective Act was passed. Although a mellower version of what she was hoping for, it was a start.

Emily had acquired a reputation as a political activist on behalf of social issues, especially those involving women and children. So when the Local Council of Women attended court one day and were asked to leave because the situation being discussed was deemed "too rough for the ears of 'decent women,'" they approached Emily with their story. The case being discussed when they were asked to leave was about a prostitute. To Emily, it didn't make sense that women in the courtroom were asked to leave while men judged a case involving a woman. In her mind, it made more sense that a woman judge should preside over these kinds of issues. And when she approached the Attorney General about the matter, he, surprisingly, agreed. He organized a women's court and appointed Emily the first female police magistrate in Alberta and the British Empire in 1916.

On her first day on the job as a police magistrate, Judge Emily found another horrible display of inequality in the political system. After making a ruling against an individual who appeared before her, the lawyer for the defendant argued that since Emily wasn't a person, any ruling she made against his client wasn't binding. His argument was based on an 1867 decision by an English court that stated, "Women are persons in matters of pains and penalties, but are not persons in matters of rights and privileges." Although the law had become obsolete in the country that initiated it, when it came to certain matters involving the Canadian government, the suggestion that women were not persons limited them.

The Supreme Court of Alberta overruled the lawyer's complaints and reinforced Emily's appointment, but it wouldn't be the last time she'd be faced with that particular argument. Her position as a police magistrate increased her profile so much so that when a position on the Senate opened up in Ottawa in 1921, the NCW called for Emily's appointment, stressing that their entire 450,000 membership all supported her name being put forward for the position. Having a woman appointed to the Senate was crucial if women were to be fairly treated since, until 1970, it was the Senate that approved divorces and made decisions on other family matters.

Emily soon discovered, however, that according to the government of Canada, it was impossible for her to be named as a senator because "women are not persons as defined by Section 24 of the BNA Act, therefore are not eligible to be senators." It was the same argument regurgitated over and over again from 1920 to 1927 until finally, Emily had had enough.

By 1916 women had won the right to vote; in 1917 the Alberta Legislature saw its first female MLA in the person of Louise McKinney; Nellie McClung was elected as a Liberal MLA in 1921; and that same year Irene Parlby won her seat for the United Farmers of Alberta political party at the Alberta Legislature. It seemed women were "person" enough to make strides in law, medicine, education and other areas of politics, yet they were not "person" enough to stand for Senate. It made no sense, and Emily was determined to tackle the issue.

It was her brother, a lawyer in Ontario, who came cross an obscure clause that said, "any five persons acting as a unit could petition the Supreme Court for an interpretation of any part of the constitution. What's more, the costs of the appeal would be covered by the Federal Department of Justice if it were judged to be of sufficient national importance."

Emily had her loophole. And she knew the perfect four women to ask to join her in her five-person quest.

In 1927, when Emily was organizing her plan to approach the federal government about this issue, Nellie McClung had served a term as MLA, was a well-known writer, a social and political activist, a diehard prohibitionist and an advocate for women's rights. It was largely through Nellie's efforts, and a stellar performance as Premier Duff Roblin at Winnipeg's Walker Theatre, bringing so much attention to the subject of a woman's right to vote, that two years later Manitoba became the first province to pass legislation on the matter. Nellie was smart, knew how to garner attention and had a lot of spunk.

Emily had already contacted Henrietta Muir Edwards on the Dower Act, and Emily knew Henrietta's keen understanding of the law would come in handy if the five women were to be successful in their bid.

Louise McKinney was the first woman to hold the position of MLA in Alberta and, in fact, the entire British Empire. She was zealous in her fight for prohibition and, because a woman's vote was desperately needed in this cause, she was also a steadfast suffragette.

Irene Parlby's concerns for women and children were ironically what propelled her into politics. A happily married wife and mother, she struggled each time she left her home and family for her political duties as MLA, but she fought ardently for social justice and "helped push through 18 bills to improve the plight of women and children."

Emily was happy with her choices. She arranged for all five to meet at her home in Edmonton and carefully crafted the following two questions:

Is power vested in the Governor General in Council of Canada, of the Parliament of Canada, or either of them, to appoint a female to the Senate of Canada? Secondly, is it constitutionally possible for the Parliament of Canada under the provisions of the British North America Act, or otherwise, to make provision for the appointment of a female to the Senate of Canada?

The questions purposefully skirted the use of the word "persons," opting instead to ask straightforwardly if a female could be appointed to the Senate and if not, what could be done about it. All five women signed their name to the document, and it was sent off on August 27, 1927.

The issue was debated, and the House of Commons and the government, once again pointing to the BNA Act, decided that it did not have the power to appoint women to the Senate. The matter was, however, forwarded to the Supreme Court of Canada by the Minister of Justice Ernest Lapointe "as an act of justice to the women of Canada." But before sending the question, the wording had been changed to, "Does the word 'persons' in Section 24 of the BNA Act include female persons?"

Emily was angry by the change—angrier still when on March 14, 1928, a Supreme Court convened for a hearing, not a trial. On April 24, 1928, Chief Justice Anglin declared it was "...of the opinion that women are not eligible for appointment by the Governor General to the Senate of Canada under Section 24 of the British North American Act, 1867, because they are not 'qualified persons' within the meaning of that section. The question submitted, understood as above indicated, will, accordingly, be answered in the negative."

With a defeat at the Supreme Court level, it was time for Emily to bring out the big guns. And after much wrangling and endless letter writing, on July 22, 1929, the five lords of the Privy Council, along with the two lawyers representing the Famous Five, gathered to review the documents presented, the past laws and the pertinent legislation. It was only after reading a 20-page report outlining the process by which the Privy Council made its decision that Lord Stankey announced the verdict in front of a crowded London courtroom on October 18, 1929.

The exclusion of women from all public offices is a relic of days more barbarous than ours…The word "persons"…May include members of both sexes, and to those who ask why the word should include female, the obvious answer is why should it not. In these circumstances, the burden is upon those who deny that the word includes women to make their case.

The verdict was a victory for Emily and her four compatriots. Her next goal—an accomplishment she very much wanted to attain—was to become Canada's first woman senator. She waited for a call that never came. Whether it was sour grapes or the political stripes of the day, four months after the Privy Council decision, the federal government appointed Cairine Wilson to the vacant Senate position in 1930.

Emily was understandably disappointed. Although a woman with so many irons in the fire one would be hard pressed to imagine how she could have made time for a Senate appointment, it was an honour she earnestly desired.

Yet, Emily and her colleagues had conquered a milestone for women's rights in Canada. For her part, Emily continued on as police magistrate until 1931 when she refocused her energies on her writing and speaking engagements. She died of an apparent heart attack in her sleep on October 27, 1933, at the age of 65.

Ironically, though five feisty females from Alberta were the ones to bring reform to the Senate, it wasn't until 1979 that Martha Bielish of Warspite became the first Albertan female appointed to that honour.

CHAPTER EIGHT

Dorothy Livesay:
Poet for the People
(1909–1996)

I remember long veils of green rain
Feathered like the shawl of my grandmother–
Green from the half-green of the spring trees
Waving in the valley.

–Green Rain

THE WORD "POET" IS TYPICALLY DEFINED AS AN INDIVIDUAL "gifted in the perception and expression of the beautiful or lyrical." The innate desire to express a thought, a point of view, an observation with special consideration to words and their use, woven together with detailed description of scene, sound, smell, texture and taste of an experience, has been in evidence from history's earliest records.

It is an intimate affair where writer and words tussle with paper and pen, arguing, articulating, combating each other until some form of harmony is reached through that perfect line, that lilting stanza, that brilliant turn of phrase. An experience not unlike making love—or giving birth.

For Dorothy Kathleen Livesay, born at 116 Lansdowne Avenue in Winnipeg, Manitoba, on October 12, 1909, it was an affair that began with her birth and followed her every moment of her life. Her father, John Fredrick Bligh Livesay, was a journalist who held the challenging position of war correspondent for a time during World War I, served as manager of Western Associated Press, and in 1917 was a founding member of Canadian Press. Her mother, Florence Hamilton Randal Livesay, spent considerable time translating Ukrainian folksongs into English and worked as a freelance writer with a love for literature.

To say Dorothy was precocious is an understatement. With an environment that sympathized with the literati, routinely entertaining the likes of Charles G.D. Roberts and E.J. Pratt, and a family with firm views on the socio-political climate of the country and the world at that time, it's no wonder Dorothy developed into one of Canada's most renowned poets.

I suppose (Florence) showed me the printed words long before I could read them, but an impression was made on me and I became conscious of what my imagination envisioned...It must be the same for children who grow up in a musical family, or who have parents with as strong an interest and involvement in sports. My education in writing owes much to my parents; writing was their world and it became mine.

Beyond that of conversation and interaction with the literary and political influences of her day, Dorothy's home environment stimulated her ability to interact with the world around her, deepening her innate sensitivity. When Winnipeg's general strike of 1919 looked as though it could turn violent, the Livesays moved to the country. The move gave Dorothy "an experience of the uninterrupted vastness of the prairie sky, and that openness of place was to be a part of much of her writing." The move to Woodlot, the name given the Livesay family home built on a nine-acre plot of land just outside of Clarkson, Ontario, further nourished Dorothy's love of nature.

"Undoubtedly it was the freedom to enjoy rural life, which my parents accepted as a human right that developed in me a love of solitude and induced a poetic sensibility."

Although environment and experience obviously enhance an individual's ability to appreciate and understand the arts, it does not make a poet. For that, Dorothy's unique ability to feel, empathize and absorb deeply through all her senses, coupled with a love of language, set the foundation for her eventual status as one of "the leading Canadian poets of the 20th Century."

Not unlike the relationship between poet and subject, Dorothy tussled and struggled with who she was, with her distinct social views and with her need to make a difference in her world.

She frequently referred to herself as a "free thinker," and she wasn't afraid to challenge the political status quo of the day or question her staunch Anglican upbringing. She constantly re-evaluated herself, her sexuality and her role as a woman in society and endlessly evolved as a person and a poet. She describes these stages of her life as "enclosed in a series of Chinese boxes. Each one taken by itself seems to have no significance; but when fitted, each within the next size, a pattern is visualized, and there is a sense of completion. So it has been with my desire to live fully, overflowing into friendships of all kinds, and at the same time to put it down. Out of experience to create something new."

Dorothy's poetic gifts appeared early. When she was 13 years old, her mother reportedly submitted some of Dorothy's work to the *Vancouver Province* for publication, marking her first sale as a writer and earning her the princely sum of $2.00. But Dorothy struggled with her natural inclination to write poetry and, for some time, she tried to refocus her literary efforts in the direction of journalism, writing articles "decrying the lack of government action to improve living standards, as well as propagandist pieces of a left-wing nature."

Her concern for the poor, the disenfranchised and the downtrodden initially motivated her towards a career in social work in Englewood, New Jersey, following her graduation from the University of Toronto. It was through her work that she witnessed first-hand the poverty and oppression of blacks living in the ghetto. As biographer Peter Stevens explains, "In a way, her stay in the United States was instrumental in her coming to terms with the problem of how to write socially conscious poetry."

It was also during this time when, as she was perusing various bookstores in New York and Greenwich Village, that Dorothy was introduced to the MacSpaunday group, "and their poetry, with its vigorous call to arms for a social revolution, rang sympathetically in her ears. She was also influenced by Day Lewis' *A Hope for Poetry* (1934), a book that evoked an optimism for the future of poetry, merging personal lyrical modes with political thought."

These experiences, coupled with her own personal, growing awareness of social concerns, resulted in her writing verse with pointed criticism. She had found a voice that could, potentially, reach out to the masses, and she used the medium relentlessly. In her poem *New Jersey, 1935*, Dorothy recounts an incident where she is discovered visiting with a black co-worker and confronted by her landlady. Disgusted by what she feels is an insult, her landlady challenges Dorothy on how she'd dare bring a "coloured girl" into her home. "For that I could whack the liver out of anyone. Don't ever let a nigger enter my door again," the landlady warned. Dorothy didn't hide her own disgust.

"'Why no! I never will—nor a white girl, either.' And I went upstairs to pack…"

Her concern for the socio-political state of her world went beyond the written word. She was part of the growing left-wing movement in Canada, was a member of the Progressive Art Club, the Young Communist League and later joined the Canadian League Against War and Fascism.

But it was through her writing that she brought those concerns to the general public most vividly, spurring her on to produce a series of socially conscious poetry. *Day and Night* and *West Coast: 1943*, for example, dealt with the Great Depression. *Call My People Home*, a documentary about the internment of more than 23,000 Japanese-Canadians by the federal government following the bombing of Pearl Harbour, was written for radio and eventually aired on CBC Radio in 1949 and 1952.

She explains in her book, *Self-Completing Tree*, how she identified herself "with a whole world movement of poets writing politically oriented social criticism and was fired with the desire to set down what was happening to my Canadian generation, historically and socially."

And she wanted her poetry to be remembered as the "expression of [her] most passionate concerns: the danger of nuclear war, the plight of women politically and socially, the mistreatment of children, and the need for improved health and dietary standards in the Third World. Whether a leap is possible, a miracle of changed feeling, changed thinking—that is the theme of many of these poems."

In the end, her focus on the world didn't negate her focus on the individual, with a good portion of her poetry dealing specifically with issues such as sexuality, life, birth, aging and death. It is only through understanding who we are and what makes us tick that we can, perhaps, begin to crawl out beyond our small worlds and make a difference. For Dorothy Livesay, a poet is constantly reinventing herself, and that's exactly what she tried to do.

Among her numerous accolades, Livesay was awarded the Governor General's Award and received several honorary degrees. She held positions of either professor or writer in residence at several universities, including the University of Manitoba, University of New Brunswick, University of Alberta, University of Toronto and Simon Fraser University. She died in Victoria, BC, in 1996.

CHAPTER NINE

Charlotte Whitton:
No Holds Barred
(1896–1975)

Only representation in the House of Commons and the Senate will afford women direct contact with national action. For this, the women of Canada must stand; for this they must strive, if they desire any other office than that of "Ladies' Aid"…it therefore becomes the duty of every Canadian woman…to prepare herself for worthy citizenship. Never in any land has the need for intelligent womanhood been so great as in the Dominion of Canada today. And never has the opportunity for woman's service been as wide and glorious.

–Charlotte Whitton, 1919

CHARLOTTE ELIZABETH HAZELTYNE WHITTON WAS BORN IN Renfrew, Ontario, on March 8, 1896, and it was clear from the start that the headstrong youngster would forge her own path in the world. When her mother decided to return to the Roman Catholic Church of her youth, Charlotte rebelled. Charlotte and her siblings had been raised in the Anglican church, and even though Charlotte's refusal to accept her mother's decision effectively split the family in two, she dug in her heels and remained Anglican. Charlotte followed the voice of her conscience, and she was content to do so.

Charlotte's strong academic performance in school, which earned her numerous monetary awards, including the T.A. Low medal as the 1914 "student of distinction" in her graduating year, gave her the financial assistance needed to attend Queen's University in Kingston, Ontario. It was while at university that Charlotte made her first mark as a woman in a traditionally male-dominated world of sports such as field hockey, ice hockey and basketball and by being elected to the prestigious appointment as the "first woman assistant editor of Queen's *Journal*." She used her position to expose her views on the social concerns of the day. In a November 1917 editorial she wrote:

Were Socrates to emerge on the campus today he would be an inmate of the House of Industry in a fortnight and Demosthenes, arrested for vagrancy on the seashore. We seem to have lost sight of the ideals which lighten all things and concentrate on mere practicalities…As a result our lives rotate on the axis of self and self advancement. We are pledged to making a living, not making a life…Because we succeed, we are satisfied and happy—and therefore circumscribed by the narrowness of our desires…there is stagnation—the stagnation of success.

Charlotte graduated from her Bachelor of Arts program with a Master of Arts in English, History and Philosophy—the advanced degree was conferred on graduates with exceptionally high marks. She decided to seek work in the field of what was then termed the "helping professions" and took her first post as the assistant secretary with the Social Service Council of Canada (SSCC) in Toronto. From 1918 until 1922, her main duties included organizational and clerical work, as well as attending "charity and child welfare conferences at the municipal and provincial level." She served on several standing committees, including "Political Purity and the Franchise," "Family Life" and "Motion Pictures and Censorship" during her four-year tenure with the SSCC.

Thought of as progressive in many of her concerns, Charlotte's views were often conflicting. On one hand, she fought for improved child welfare policies and equality for women, but on other issues she was less understanding. In one report that highlighted what Charlotte called the "immigration problem," she suggested that "the high percentage of 'feebleminded' immigrant girls who went into domestic service probably accounted for the high percentage of illegitimate births among them."

It was while working at the SSCC that Charlotte met Margaret Grier. Margaret worked with the juvenile court, the Girl Guides and the Big Sisters

Association. The two women, though drastically different in their personalities, formed a deep friendship that resulted in their living together in what was deemed as a "Bostonian marriage"— a term used in the late 19th century to describe "a long-term monogamous relationship between two unmarried women, most likely feminists, who were financially independent of men either through inheritance or career."

Since women typically earned far less than their male counterparts, this kind of living arrangement was a socially acceptable practice of the day, and the two women moved to Ottawa where Charlotte became the founding director of the Canadian Council on Child Welfare (CCCW), a position she held from 1920 to 1941.

The formation of the CCCW grew out of the SSCC's desire to see the development of a "children's bureau for Canada." Initially, Charlotte was involved with the organization as an honorary secretary since its inception in 1920. She received $500 a year as an honorarium for her work, which included everything from writing reports on child labour laws and analyzing the Juvenile Delinquent Act of 1908 to mailing pre- and post-natal brochures and diet folders. She worked evenings and weekends and maintained a day job at the same time. It wasn't until 1926 that the organization had sufficient funds to pay an executive administrative officer and support staff. By then

Charlotte's role was cemented, and she travelled Canada's north to the British Columbia coastline to see for herself the social needs of Canadians in less affluent parts of the country.

While Charlotte was seemingly content with her career path, she struggled with the expectation of the day that a young lady should marry and settle down. And although she was a staunch advocate for women's rights and believed equal pay for equal work was only right, she also decried women who wanted both worlds—to marry and have a career.

Charlotte had at least two serious suitors who asked for her hand in marriage, but she was infinitely more comfortable focusing on her career and, in the end, on her relationship with Margaret. Charlotte was generally more at ease with women, and although any suggestion that she and Margaret had a physical relationship is purely speculation, it was clear there was a deep love between them. In the end, Charlotte turned down her suitors and refocused her attention on child welfare advocacy, the plight of illegitimate children, unwed mothers and other social issues. By doing so she remained independent—a decision she would later reinforce with her statement, "There are two categories of women: those who are women and those who are men's wives."

Charlotte left the CCCW in 1941 and spent the next nine years writing reports, conducting studies and lecturing across Canada and the United States as she struggled to redefine her career goals.

Her contributions weren't always welcomed. Such was the case in 1945 when she approached Alberta's Premier Ernest Manning, leader of the province's Social Credit Party at that time, after the Edmonton chapter of the Imperial Order of Daughters of the Empire (IODE) shared concerns among the province's social workers. The IODE wanted Charlotte to conduct a social survey similar to those conducted by the Canadian Welfare Council in 1929, 1931 and 1944. Manning declined government approval, and Charlotte explained to the IODE that she was unwilling to proceed with the survey without it. But after a second interview with Manning a year later, she explained she would conduct a "study"—though she didn't clearly explain the difference between the two. Manning refused government approval again, but in January 1947 Charlotte went ahead with it anyway. She hoped the gamble would pay off with national publicity focused on the problems in the province and force the government of the day to make reforms.

In an April 21 news release entitled "Some Wrongs That Need Righting," Charlotte attacked the government's care for the mentally handicapped and its services for children and the aged. In one correspondence with the State Child Welfare Division of Montana, Charlotte called Alberta's child placement practices "fast and loose adoption traffic, largely carried on by one official and notorious in Western Canada." These reports put Alberta under a magnifying glass, and local and national media outlets were scrambling for a peek of their own. Charlotte was hailed as "Canada's First Lady of Social Service Work," but she'd have to defend her findings to a royal commission.

In the midst of the upheaval, tragedy struck her personal life when Margaret fell ill and, after two surgeries, continued to weaken. Charlotte rushed home to her side, but Margaret and her doctor convinced her to return to Alberta because of the serious nature of the work she was doing there. Margaret died on December 9, 1947, and although Charlotte had left Alberta to see her friend, she didn't make it in time.

Margaret's death was perhaps the most crushing blow in Charlotte's life. In a letter to Mrs. G. Sheane, a member of the Calgary Canadian Women's Club, Charlotte shared her pain:

It is she who suffered most from this particular work of mine…She faced the final crossing over without me when we had never taken but one holiday apart in our 30 years of life together. It will have to be a great good for the children of Alberta that ultimately results to compensate for that in the final days here of a woman as fine as Margaret Grier.

Charlotte's work in Alberta did produce "a great good for the children" of that province, but she

would forever grieve what she viewed as her aban-
donment of a dear friend in her time of need.

For a time, Charlotte provided regular copy as a
syndicated columnist for the Ottawa *Evening Citi-
zen*. She also wrote regular columns for the Thom-
son Dailies and the Halifax *Chronicle-Herald*. The
columns gave her a venue to air her feminist views,
her concerns regarding the aged, rent controls and
child desertion, as well as financial stability.

In 1950, with help from a small army of women
nicknamed Ottawa's "Petticoat Brigade," Charlotte
was elected as Ottawa's first woman controller in
the civic government. Shortly thereafter she
became acting mayor following the death of
Mayor Grenville Goodwin. In 1951 she was
named unanimously as Ottawa's first woman
mayor—an honour that brought with it the added
distinction of being the first woman mayor ever to
be elected in a major Canadian city.

Charlotte was re-elected in 1952 and 1954, but
did not seek re-election in 1956. Instead, she
bowed out of civic politics with a new goal in
mind—to seek election to the federal government.
In 1957 Charlotte sought the Progressive Conservative nomination in the riding of Ottawa West.
She won out against her opponent, Osmond F.
Howe, QC, with 1666 votes to his 350, and
declared, "Oh, yes! This old girl has been around
a long time and run up quite a mileage, but she's
still going strong."

It was a victory to be proud of, but one that was short-lived. Charlotte lost the 1958 federal election with an astounding 17,397 votes to Liberal Party candidate George McIllraith's 18,431. Only a thousand votes separated the two frontrunners, but Charlotte wasn't to be comforted. Nearing her 60th birthday, Charlotte recognized that a bid for a federal government seat in the future was less likely with each passing year. Weighing her options, she decided to run for mayor again in 1960 and 1962 and was victorious both times.

During her reign as mayor, Charlotte was known for her sharp tongue, caustic comments and occasional physical flare-ups. A media account as far away as Johannesburg reported one such explosion where, shortly after Charlotte was re-elected mayor in 1962, she'd "given a thorough foot and fist drubbing to a fellow council member." In another instance, when it was suggested a certain discussion wasn't fitting in front of a lady and should be diverted because Charlotte was in attendance, her response was, "Whatever my sex, I'm no lady."

While Charlotte may have entered her sixth decade, she hadn't mellowed with age. As feisty and flamboyant as ever, she headed into yet another mayoral race in 1964. This time, however, she was defeated by city controller Don Reid who had 43,854 votes to her 23,858.

Charlotte refused to see the defeat as the final chapter of her public life. Instead, not quite 70, she continued to write and lecture and even announced that she was "ready and willing to be prime minister." In 1966 she re-entered civic politics, running as alderman for the city of Ottawa, and maintained that position for the next five years, proving herself as staunch an opponent as ever.

Ottawa's flamboyant mayor and long-time alderman, who provided top-notch copy for reporters and kept her colleagues on their toes, would likely have worked to her last day had it not been for a fall in 1972 that resulted in a serious hip fracture. For the next three years Charlotte was in and out of hospitals and homes for the aged, frustrated over her own lack of ability to regain her strength. She died on January 25, 1975, just a few weeks after suffering a heart attack.

Throughout her life, Charlotte acquired many accolades. She was voted Canada's "Woman of the Year" six times and received the honour of being named an Officer of the Order of Canada in April 1968.

It was Charlotte who coined the phrase, "Whatever women do they must do twice as well as men to be thought half as good. Luckily, this is not difficult," and it was a sentiment she was determined to prove to her dying day.

CHAPTER TEN

Anne Adamson Campbell:
The Sound of Music
(1912–)

*Music has a power of forming the character,
and should therefore be introduced into the
education of the young.*

—Aristotle

WHEN ANNE ADAMSON CAME INTO THE WORLD ON JUNE 16,
1912, her first cry was music to her parents' ears.
The newlyweds, having married just a couple of
years earlier, had left their Scottish homeland and
crossed the Atlantic Ocean in search of new
opportunities in a new land. They first settled in
Winnipeg, then moved on to Sutherland—a small
community near Saskatoon. With a baby to consider, as with any new parents, the couple wanted
to give her the very best upbringing possible.

For the Adamson clan, the gift of music was perhaps the most valuable provision Anne could have
received.

"My father and mother had good voices. Mom
sang in the church choir. Dad was a tenor and sang

lots around the house. When people came to visit us, there was always singing around the piano."

Singing in the church choir was something all the Adamsons did. By the age of eight, Anne had already begun taking formal singing lessons, travelling each week to Saskatoon by bus, and by 14, she took her first official steps into what would become her life's work by conducting the St. Paul's United Church Junior Choir.

After years of study, Anne earned her certificate as an Associate of the Royal Conservatory of Music (ARCT), another as an Associate in Music (A.Mus) and a Licentiate in Music in piano (L.Mus).

In 1939 Anne married Don Campbell at the Westminister United Church in Saskatoon. The couple moved to Calgary, and Anne settled into family life, focusing on raising her two sons Mac (1943) and Stewart (1947), but her love for music never waned. Even with two youngsters, Anne continued to teach voice, piano and musical theory, and she frequently performed at the Wesley United Church, at the same time continuing her own studies in voice.

Before long the young family was on the move again, first to Picture Butte and then to Lethbridge, Alberta, in 1953, where the family settled for more than three decades. Don had purchased a hardware store, and Anne busied herself with her family and, of course, with her music.

Much of my time was devoted to music-making, teaching and solo work. Our home was constantly full of children having music lessons or practicing. My choirs sometimes rehearsed in the basement studio at our house. Most weeks, 60 or more children came in and out of the house.

While it was obvious that music made her world go round, Anne likely didn't envision where her energies would eventually take her—and how on hearing her all-girls choirs were going to perform in this town or another, people would come from miles around to fill the seats wherever they were playing.

The first choir she formed in Lethbridge was the Junior Girls Choir. As her young choir grew, it became apparent another group was necessary, and by 1963 she'd formed the Teen-Clefs, followed by the Anne Campbell Singers in 1968. If that wasn't enough, Anne added a Mini Choir to her commitments, working with girls aged six to eight years. And for the ladies who'd graduated, Anne added the Linnet Singers to her more than full plate.

Every year brought with it a new production season for each group. Her Junior Girls Choir was affiliated with the Southminister United Church, and as such, she scheduled them to sing once a month during the Sunday service. These girls also held a fall operetta, and all the choirs learned new material for the Spring Sing concert, the Kiwanis

Music Festivals in Lethbridge, Medicine Hat, Card-
ston, Crowsnest Pass and Calgary, and they even
competed at the provincial and national level.

"We were very proud to be invited to sing at
Expo '67, 'Terre des Hommes' for the Montreal
Universal and International Exhibition of 1967.
The Teen Clefs also sang at the Centenary Festi-
vals of Music in Saint John, New Brunswick, in
July 1967."

These two trips were such a success that Anne
knew they were ready to enter international competition. Her first stop was a 1968 tour with 55
girls to "compete at the Tees-side International
Eisteddfod Festival in Middlesborough, Yorkshire
and the Llangollen International Musical
Eisteddfod in Wales."

The senior girls took first place in the female
choir category and the junior girls "received the
highest points ever awarded at the Bournemouth
Music Competitions Festival." Her girls had made
it in the big leagues. They held one homecoming
performance after another, a competition here and
another there. In the end, one or another of
Anne's groups, dressed in official Albertan tartan,
had performed in England, Scotland, Ireland,
Wales, Germany, Denmark, Belgium, Austria,
Japan and throughout Canada. The Anne Campbell Singers also produced 13 albums for three different record companies, and the Linnet Singers
recorded one album.

In 1976 Anne was recognized for her commitment to music excellence when she received the Governor General's medal. In 1978 she was also awarded the Silver Medal from Queen Elizabeth, and in 1983 she was given a Doctor of Laws Honoris Causa by the University of Lethbridge.

But Anne is quick to add that she was never in the business of seeking out personal accolades.

My biggest reward is knowing that hundreds of young girls became successful, music-enriched adults and parents. I love to see my former singers and their babies. I know of many singers who took their first training from me and are now pursuing professional careers in music and music education…I am one of those fortunate people who has had the thrill of doing exactly what I enjoyed the most, fulfilling my purpose in life at the same time. For that, I am grateful, and I would do it all over again if I had the chance.

CHAPTER ELEVEN

Charlotte Ross:
Medical Maverick
(1843–1916)

"All aboard!" Was it not just a few moments ago that the train conductor gave that familiar last boarding call, and already home seemed like a thousand miles away? A young Charlotte Ross shook her head in disbelief. The journey she'd pondered and prayed over was now, finally, after five long years of preparation, taking place. It would be another 25 hours before she reached her destination via train and steamship. At the age of 27, Charlotte was doing what most would frown on, if not totally condemn—she was leaving her home to study medicine at the Women's Medical College of Pennsylvania. It was something she needed to do—was born to do. Still, she knew her heart remained in Montreal, with her husband and their three children.

CHARLOTTE WHITEHEAD WAS BORN IN 1843, THE THIRD CHILD of Joseph and Isabella Whitehead. Joseph brought his family from England to British North America in 1849, and the family settled in a place called The Corners, which later became the town of Clinton,

Ontario, just a stone's throw from the southeastern tip of Lake Huron. Joseph, who was elected as an officer of the town council, served as its first reeve and was elected as an opposition member for the coalition government of Sir John A. Macdonald at Confederation. It's no accident, then, that Charlotte's stepmother, Margaret, frequently compared the temperament of the daughter to the father. And it's also no accident that Charlotte's inherent determination would bode well for her entry into what was then a men's-only profession.

Charlotte's decision to study medicine was a direct result of personal experience. Her mother and younger brother died within three weeks of each other when Charlotte was eight years old. And for most of her life she helped care for her older sister, Mary Anne, who suffered from "weak lungs." When Mary Anne died at the age of 28, leaving behind a husband and two small children, Charlotte was more determined than ever to do all that was humanly possible to become a doctor and devote her life to bringing hope to the sick and suffering.

A strong-minded woman, Charlotte's very presence commanded respect. At a time when even the thought of a woman studying medicine was laughable, Charlotte had at least two prominent male physicians in her corner.

Dr. Cole, the Whitehead family physician, encouraged Charlotte's inquisitive mind by providing her with reading materials that included a copy of Da Costa's *Practice of Medicine*. By studying that book as she sat with her sister through the last five months of her illness, she learned Mary Anne had what was referred to as consumption. And although Dr. Cole didn't agree with a woman becoming a doctor, he did concede that Charlotte would make a good doctor.

It was Charlotte's friendship with Dr. William Hales Hingston, a prominent "Montréal surgeon and a founding member of the Canadian Medical Association," that was perhaps her most valuable asset. Not only did Hingston provide her with reading material, such as Scanzoni's *Diseases of Women*, but the glowing reference he wrote surely aided in her admission to the Women's Medical College in Pennsylvania.

Shortly after Mary Anne's death in 1869, Charlotte discussed her plans to apply for medical school with her stepmother. Margaret knew Charlotte's father would be angry about the idea, and the fact that no Canadian medical schools accepted women students would necessitate Charlotte's travelling to the U.S. to study, but Margaret remained a solid moral support for Charlotte.

Margaret was supportive in another way, too. She contacted two aunts living in Philadelphia, and as a result, Charlotte had a place to call home while she was away from her husband David Ross and their three children. Aunt Annie and Aunt

Johan—two Quaker women who belonged to the Religious Society of Friends—were progressive thinkers and supported equal rights for women. It was this organization that was partly responsible for the founding of the first medical school for women in North America in 1850.

David and Charlotte had married in 1861, and despite the fact that David was always supportive of his wife's endeavours, Charlotte elected to keep her plans to attend medical school to herself until she received notification that she'd been admitted. When the letter arrived, Charlotte broke the news to her husband, telling him she'd received something of importance in the post. Charlotte's news that she'd been accepted to medical school probably worried David, but as always he was supportive. In fact, he was surprised that it had taken his wife so long to finally decide to go. It was so like her husband to support her efforts at all costs.

Still, she was torn with her calling and the lonely ache she was already feeling, knowing she'd be separated from her family for almost half the year, for three years. It was decided that David's mother would care for their children during Charlotte's absence. David's Scottish heritage and its respect for scholarly endeavours was perhaps one reason he and his family readily accepted Charlotte's decision to leave her duties in the home to study in a traditionally male-dominated field.

When Charlotte left for Philadelphia that fall day in 1870, her daughter Bella, just eight at the time, wanted desperately to join her mother. Her other daughters, Kate and Min, were a little younger, and Charlotte found waving goodbye to her family at the train station heart-wrenching.

But when she discovered early into the fall session that she was pregnant again, it felt as if a part of her family was still with her. She was overjoyed with the situation, but the long hours of study resulted in the loss of the baby just before the Christmas break, and Charlotte left school to recover from the subsequent complications. Charlotte's father thought the miscarriage was proof that studying medicine was too difficult for women, who are "emotionally and physically incapable of coping with the stress involved in the study and practice of medicine."

But her husband stood by her decision to reapply in the fall of 1871. "We all know you have difficulty carrying babies to full term," David said, trying to comfort his wife and reassure her of her decision to return to school.

Charlotte recognized that the pain of leaving everyone behind would be too much for her to bear, and when she finally returned to school she took Kate and Min with her. She succeeded in completing her first year, but when she discovered she was again pregnant, she postponed her second year of study, only to return with Min and seven-month-old Carrie in the fall of 1873.

Having postponed her studies twice, she decided to continue through another pregnancy during her third and final year at school, and after five years of interrupted study, she graduated in 1875. Charlotte hadn't expected David to attend her convocation because he was extremely busy with his work, but she was visibly pleased when he arrived and embraced her, calling her Dr. Charlotte Ross.

Charlotte was one of 57 women enrolled in the Women's Medical College of Pennsylvania in the fall of 1870. Dr. Ann Preston, a lifelong advocate for medical education for women and the first woman to hold the position of college dean, greeted her eager students with the harsh realities that not only was this path a tough row to hoe, but that the women would have to work much harder than their male counterparts and work at a consistently higher level to succeed. It was an admonishment that prepared Charlotte well for study—and the development of her practice.

Her first order of business, after she opened her Montréal office, was to apply for admission to the Québec College of Physicians and Surgeons. Her application wasn't received seriously. Dr. Robert Russell, the president of the organization, refused to greet her as Dr. Charlotte Ross and declared, "In mind, emotions and physical makeup, a woman is not suited to the practice of medicine. In matters of morals and modesty, a lady certainly isn't."

Noticing she was pregnant, he went further, suggesting she go home and have her baby. "No doubt your medical training will equip you better to care for your family."

Charlotte had expected such a reaction. She merely approached it as a matter of record. Her next stop was to Dr. Hingston's office. Hingston, newly elected as mayor of Montréal, acted as her ally until her move to Manitoba.

While Charlotte continued to practise in the Québec city, despite constant threats of fines and jail terms, it wasn't until she settled with her family in their new home in Whitemouth, Manitoba, in 1881 that she began to feel she could provide a truly valuable service. Pioneering the West was a challenge for the men who were attempting to tame that wild land. It was even more challenging for the women who followed them. For Charlotte—the first white woman to arrive and settle in Whitemouth—the challenge was even greater. She took on the roles of a wife and mother, as well as being the only doctor caring for the mill workers, rail workers and farmers in Whitemouth and for miles around.

While David secured a livelihood for his family, purchasing timber rights and operating a sawmill, Charlotte began to make a home for her family and was expecting the couple's sixth child. Since they were living in an area populated by men, Charlotte didn't think she'd be practising medicine officially until wives and children began arriving at their small settlement. So when one of David's employees arrived at the family home, calling Charlotte to come to the aid of a sick man, she was surprised—but, as always, prepared.

"He's over here." Charlotte nodded in the direction of the voice calling her from a corner of her husband's office. David introduced his wife as the doctor. Peter Hall was one very sick young man, but his first thought was simply, "She's a woman!"

In a firm but caring voice, Charlotte instructed the man to open his shirt. When he moaned, she opened the shirt for him and placed her stethoscope on his chest. She checked his temperature, his pulse, his throat, asked a series of questions and then delivered her verdict. Peter Hall had contracted rubella. Although the disease needed to be monitored, and complications could result, it was nonetheless a relief that it wasn't typhoid fever.

Sometime later, once Hall had recovered, he appeared at the Ross's front door to thank Charlotte in person. He was sporting a black eye and suggested it was the result of an altercation with a doorknob. Charlotte knew better. The young man had defended her honour and her abilities as a doctor when one of the men at his boarding house teased him that he had a woman in his room during his convalescence.

"You should have seen the other guy," Peter said. "You'll not have any trouble in these parts. And if you do, just call for me."

Another time, Charlotte was called to the aid of an accident victim. A 17-year-old man who was working as a cook's helper had split open his foot while chopping wood. The young man was transported by handcar and delivered to Charlotte's front door. It took five men to get him there, but once they arrived, Charlotte confidently took control and saved the man's life.

These two incidents served as the foundation for Charlotte's reputation as the area's doctor. She was the only doctor from Whitemouth to Winnipeg, 105 kilometres away. Between her responsibilities as a wife and mother and her role as a doctor, roles that she took equally seriously, Charlotte's life was very full indeed.

As well as fighting for equality in a male-dominated profession, Charlotte was well beyond her time as a medical doctor. She recognized, long before it became vogue, that caring for patients meant meeting more than just their physical needs; it also must incorporate their mental, spiritual and emotional well-being—something she demonstrated repeatedly.

An illustration of this is when Charlotte delivered baby number 11 to a young, struggling immigrant family. Although not the poorest of her patients, this family made their home in a one-room, rough-hewn cabin. The family's diet consisted mainly of rabbit and sturgeon from the nearby Whitemouth River, and there wasn't a frivolous, beautiful thing to be seen in the entire home. A day or so after the birth, Charlotte checked in on her patient, bringing with her a bouquet of her very own roses to set at the mother's bedside—something cheerful and fragrant for her to enjoy.

She also brought loaves of her freshly made bread, a roast of beef, potatoes and vegetables, and asked the eldest daughter if she could prepare a beef stew. As a treat, Charlotte brought out 10 apples—one for each of the older children—and some of her own handmade items from her last child's baby layette.

Such was the life and style of Charlotte Ross. She was a woman who fought hard for the people she cared for.

She eventually sought the counsel of a lawyer to assist her in petitioning the Manitoba legislature to award her a licence to practise medicine legally in the province. Charlotte knew she could have re-entered medical school in Canada, since by that time they were accepting women students, but she would not, reasoning that she was forced to spend the time and expense of travelling to another country to obtain her medical degree, and it should be recognized.

The Manitoba government refused to give her the recognition she sought, but she continued to care for the people on the undulating prairies of the lake district of Manitoba for another 25 years. She retired from practice in 1912 at the age of 69 and died in 1916.

Today, the community of Whitemouth honours the first woman doctor in Manitoba who served its pioneers with such dedication. Her name is revered in tourist pamphlets and on area websites. As one website acknowledges, "She defied the so-called establishment and got on with her work, only to be legitimized posthumously in March 1993."

CHAPTER TWELVE

Muriel McQueen Fergusson:
No Time to Waste
(1899–1997)

There are still more areas to be conquered and more battles to be won...

–Muriel McQueen Fergusson

MURIEL MCQUEEN ENTERED THE WORLD AT A TIME WHEN THE Victorian ideal for respectable young ladies was to focus their life's work and education on becoming model wives and mothers. Born on May 26, 1899, in Shediac, New Brunswick, Muriel made it quite clear from an early age that she had ideas of her own. When Muriel's brother was born in 1903, Muriel decided his name should be Tommy, after the soldier in Rudyard Kipling's poem of the same name. Tommy Atkins was her hero, and even after Muriel's brother had been baptized Robert Arthur, he was always Tommy to her.

It's not surprising then, as a young woman destined, in her mother's mind, to attend Ladies College, that Muriel had other plans. Her school marks were strong, and Muriel wanted more than an education in elocution. Muriel wasn't inconsiderate of her mother's wishes, however, and initially attempted a dual-study program—to complete her elocution course at Ladies College and to enroll in a regular Bachelor of Arts program at Mount Allison University in Sackville, New Brunswick. Although her plans worked for a time, Muriel missed the entire second semester of study when she went home to care for her ill mother. On returning to her studies, she tried to keep up with both programs, doubling her classes to catch up with what she'd missed. Eventually, however, she had to make a choice and, despite her mother's wishes, she decided to complete her university studies.

In the meantime, Muriel met the love of her life—a young soldier named Aubrey Stafford Fergusson, who'd returned to university after serving with the 9th Siege Battery in France. Following Aubrey's graduation from Mount Allison University in 1921, he was off to King's College in Saint John and then to Harvard to study law.

Muriel agreed to marry Aubrey at a time when combining marriage and a career were simply out of the question. And while Aubrey was away at Harvard, Muriel was determined to complete her own law degree at Dalhousie University. Her mother thought the idea a frivolous expense for a woman engaged to be married, but her father, who was a lawyer himself, supported Muriel. By 1924 Muriel finished her course of studies and spent 1925 articling in her father's office. Both Muriel and Aubrey passed the bar in 1924.

Now that Aubrey was back home, the couple married and moved to Grand Falls, New Brunswick, to run a law practice for the father of a friend of Aubrey's from Mount Allison. Frederick Kertson had approached Aubrey after his father had suffered a heart attack. He promised Aubrey that he would be made a partner in his father's firm if his father recovered enough to return to work. If he did not, Aubrey could arrange to take over the practice. Kertson's father passed away soon after, and Aubrey and Muriel took over the practice, working together until Aubrey's death in 1942.

Although Muriel didn't experience discrimination in the workplace from her husband, it took a while before she achieved the same respect from Audrey's male clients when she took over the practice. The world at this time was wading its way through another war, and Muriel accepted a job with the Wartime Prices and Trade Board. She was also involved in several women's groups, writing and delivering speeches across New Brunswick.

Once the war was over, it was clear to Muriel that her job with the Wartime Prices and Trade Board would end, and it was time to start looking for other work. The new family allowance program had been operating in Fredericton for about a year by that time, and the position of program director was open—a position Muriel was more than qualified for. Muriel applied, but the advertisement for the job stated only men would be considered for the position. The situation rankled

her, and she wasn't about to let the issue go without a fight. Reflecting on the problem during one
interview, Muriel outlined her plan of attack:

*I had quite a few connections through the University
Women's Club, through the Business and Professional
Women's Club, through the Women's Council, so I alerted
the national offices and we started sending protests in.
Not about me, but because that position which a woman
was quite capable of handling was advertised only for
men. And that it should be open as an opportunity for
women too. Women could do that job.*

Their collective voice was heard, the job was
advertised again—this time without the reference
to male-only applicants—and Muriel found herself
appointed as the first woman director of the New
Brunswick family allowance program. In time, the
old age security program was added to her duties
as well.

In the early 1950s Muriel moved into municipal politics and became the first woman elected to
the Fredericton city council and the first woman to
serve as deputy mayor in that city. Her mother
couldn't see much value in Muriel's work, scolding
her for spending so much time at "that job." And
despite the fact that Muriel was in her early 50s,
she told her mother that she was visiting a neighbourhood friend, Maude McKee, when she was
really going out to attend council meetings.

In 1953, Muriel received a call that changed her
life. Prime Minister Louis St. Laurent had appointed

her to the Senate—a position she filled for 22 years. On December 14, 1972, Muriel was appointed the first woman Speaker of the Senate. She continued in this role until her retirement at the age of 75.

While serving on the Senate, Muriel fought for women's rights in all areas of society. It was she who pushed for changes to the Criminal Code that would allow women to serve on juries in criminal cases.

In 1985 the Muriel McQueen Fergusson Foundation was established to recognize her commitment to social action and justice. The foundation was initially set up to "raise money and assist victims of family violence through the funding of shelters, special programs and public education projects." Since its inception, the foundation has expanded its mandate to include funding for research "into the causes, incidence and forms of treatment of family violence, and to promote and sponsor effective public education programs to counter widespread ignorance of the problem."

Whether in politics or in her private life, Muriel's tireless quest to make a difference in the world continued to her dying day, just two weeks before her 98th birthday. After all, there was still so much to do.

CHAPTER THIRTEEN

~❊~

Helen Huston:
Doctor on the Roof of the World
(1927–)

The city of Mumbai, once known as Bombay, is a modern one today. Along Marine Drive there is a winding, paved street lined with high-rise apartments to the east that kiss the Malabar Coastline and overlook the Arabian Sea to the west. Now, instead of rickshaws cluttering the roadways, foreign cars jam with pedestrians during rush hour traffic. Today, Mumbai is considered the most affluent, industrialized city in India—a city that prides itself in its blend of traditional and modern lifestyles; one that countless tourists are drawn to each year.

But in October 1953, when Dr. Helen Huston first set foot in the city, known today as the "Gateway to India," modern-day Mumbai was still in its infancy. For Dr. Helen, as she came to be known, it was the pungent aroma of spice that hung heavily in the air, the sound of chanting, holy men with long, flowing beards quietly meditating as they walked along the dirt roadways—all this and more—that greeted the

young woman from Canada. Where she would
go from here she wasn't sure. But she'd made it.

HELEN HUSTON CAME INTO THE WORLD ON THE CRISP FALL
day of September 20, 1927. As fallen leaves littered
the roads and sidewalks of the rural community
of Innisfail, Alberta, Helen's father, Will, was
preparing for Thanksgiving. Because Helen's father
was a United Church minister, her family lived in
several rural Alberta communities before she
would come of age and strike out on her own.
Although they didn't have much in the way of
material possessions or financial stability, Helen's
parents loved her, and she had a safe secure home,
three siblings to rough-house with and an unlimited future to tap into.

At the same time, Helen was her own person.
She never conformed to the public view of how a
daughter of a minister should behave. Instead, she
laughed and giggled and played ball with the boys,
enjoying all the innocence of youth.

By the time she was 12, Helen decided she
wanted to become a doctor and work as a missionary in China. But the uncertainty that comes with
the turbulent teen years had her doubting her calling, until the summer of her graduation year when
she attended a Canadian Girls in Training summer
camp at Sylvan Lake.

It was there in the summer of 1945 that she met Elda Daniels, a missionary from Korea. Although not her first exposure to the life and experiences of a missionary, Helen couldn't get enough of Elda's stories, and the interaction reopened a longing in her heart. As she walked along the shores of Sylvan Lake one evening that summer, she was so lost in thought that she didn't notice an oncoming storm. Caught in the wind and rain, Helen stopped for a moment, looked over the turbulent waters and into the horizon and called to God in prayer. She asked for direction, and in her heart she knew what she must do.

It took Helen two years to raise the money she needed for her tuition, but by the fall of 1947 she was admitted into the Faculty of Medicine at the University of Alberta—one of only four women accepted that year in a class of 55 students. It then took six, long, focused years before she reached the shores of India, but she was determined to achieve her goal.

In the fall of 1953, Helen met all the requirements necessary to merit her the title of doctor. However, once she'd received a posting, she was one of a rare few who spoke English. So Helen went back to the books before heading out into the field—she and the other missionaries arriving in India that fall spent a year in language school.

Despite her education, Helen grappled with an emptiness she couldn't explain. Although she'd been raised in a Christian family, she struggled with her faith as she worked her way through a very scientific course of study. In India, where Buddhism and Hinduism flourished, her mission- ary counterparts took solace in their personal rela- tionship with their Christian God, but Helen felt bereft of any such comfort. She felt that to be effective in her work as a medical missionary she had to come to terms with where she stood in rela- tion to her faith.

While on retreat just before the Easter weekend of 1954, Helen pondered her situation. And it was while strolling the well-manicured grounds of the retreat centre under a tree blooming with the promise of new life that Helen came to a personal faith commitment. The resultant peace that flooded her being gave her renewed strength. Regardless where she went or what she was asked to do, for the first time in her life she really knew she wasn't alone.

Of course, being human meant that, even with such a revelation, Helen was tested and tried and, from time to time, panicked at the recognition of her own limited abilities. Such was the case when she arrived at her first posting at the 35-bed hos- pital in Dhar.

With only six weeks of field training at the Indore Hospital after language school, Helen was the only physician stationed at the hospital and, therefore, had no one of equal training or more experience to consult with on difficult cases. And aside from a single lab technician, Helen was the only English-speaking person there. The medications were as foreign to her as the diseases of malaria and typhoid—tropical diseases weren't a primary focus of her Western-based medical training. Add to that the fact that the Indian doctor she was replacing informed her she was to conduct a craniotomy the following morning, and she was overwhelmed. Not only had she never performed the delicate surgery, which required that she make a surgical incision into the patient's skull, she'd never even seen it performed. Even a determined, confident, faith-filled soul like Helen had to take a moment.

The next day, much to her relief, the procedure wasn't quite what she'd expected. The doctor had used the wrong medical term. Instead of a craniotomy, Helen was to operate on a woman whose pregnancy had ended in a stillbirth because she wasn't able to deliver. Although a sad situation, it was something Helen could handle.

Over the next few months, Helen experienced the joy of seeing malnourished or sick children recover and gain strength. She also witnessed the powerful destruction of disease.

But when Helen returned to the Indore Hospital and her duties there, she found herself struggling again. In Dhar she had been the sole, available doctor, and Helen didn't feel she'd met her calling by working at the larger medical centre of Indore. So when she received a call to go to Nepal and serve, for a time, at the cholera hospital in Kathmandu, Helen felt it was an answer to her prayer.

The borders to Nepal had just opened to foreigners in 1951. Until that time, the country had been restricted to visitors. When Helen first arrived in the land-locked country of mystery in 1955, Nepal already had a population of about 8.5 million. Most of its inhabitants made a living in agriculture, a lifestyle filled with hardship. Only about 20 percent of the land was fit for farming, and without the benefits of modern agricultural practices, it was a challenge to produce the food needed to meet both domestic and export responsibilities.

In Nepal, Hinduism and Buddhism were the dominant religions. While foreigners were viewed with suspicion, Christian foreigners were even more so. Still, it was a country in desperate need of assistance.

Christian missionaries bringing schools, hospitals and agricultural and technical training could not be refused. From the time the borders were opened until today, foreign aid has been Nepal's chief source of income.

Two fellow missionaries met Helen when she arrived in Kathmandu. The trio bobbed away on rough terrain to what was known as "the old cholera hospital" at Teku. Helen was to be in charge of one portion of the hospital designated for women and children. The Ministry of Health maintained the other half in case of another cholera outbreak, which often struck in three- or four-year cycles. For three months Helen tended to the needs of her patients at the hospital and conducted community clinics with one of the staff nurses. In India, Helen had witnessed the ravages of disease and the tragedy of preventable death, but here in Nepal—a land made even more remote by its rough terrain and proximity to the Himalayas—the need seemed so much greater. Nepal captured her heart, but it would be another four years before she was permanently stationed there.

From 1960 until her retirement in 1992, Helen's focus was on the roughly 250,000 people living in the surrounding hillsides near the small, remote village of Amp Pipal, located 140 kilometres northwest of Kathmandu in the Gorkha District of Nepal. While medical help was limited in nearby Kathmandu or India, it was virtually non-existent in the remote villages. Aside from the routine injuries, fractures and burns of daily living, diseases such as tuberculosis, diphtheria and even smallpox claimed lives on a regular basis. Add to that common dysentery, and problems with labour and delivery, and the only doctor in the area didn't want for work. What she did acknowledge the need for, however, was a hospital.

"Friends…I have told you a little of the fine pioneering missionary outreach work to serve the neglected people in the hills of Nepal," the voice of

Reverend Russell Ross of the First United Church in Vancouver boomed over the radio airwaves in Canada one Sunday evening. He continued:

A hospital is desperately needed. I believe we have a unique opportunity at this time to donate money so that the mission can go ahead and build it. And I think we Western Canadians have a vested interest in this important project; the medical work is under the direction of Dr. Helen Huston from Alberta.

It was a dream that took time, prayer and the generosity of others, but by 1969 the dispensary where Helen and her skeleton medical staff worked was replaced by a hospital built from mud and stone on the slopes of the Lig Lig Mountain. The building and its new equipment was a miracle made possible largely by generous donations from individuals who had heard of Dr. Helen's work through people like Reverend Ross. Dr. Helen was thrilled. With a new hospital and equipment she'd be able to reach out to even more of the Nepalese.

But just getting to medical help was a challenge for the majority of Dr. Helen's patients. Many of the sick relied on the kindness of family and friends to make it to the hospital. In the case of 14-year-old Kiran Kumar, it took 15 men an entire day to take turns carrying the injured boy on a stretcher to the hospital. By the time he got there, the broken bones in Kiran's arms were protruding from the dirty wound. Soon he spiked a fever and complained of pain, twitching muscles and a stiff neck. Without a doubt, the young man had contracted tetanus.

Without immediate treatment, tetanus is almost always fatal. But Helen was never one to give up without a fight. She limited all sensory stimulation in the young man's vicinity, prescribed muscle relaxants, inserted a stomach tube for feeding in case Kiran developed lockjaw, administered an anti-tetanus serum—which wasn't administered earlier because the family insisted he'd been inoculated at birth—and gave him antibiotics. For some time Kiran hovered between life and death. Powerful muscle spasms contracted and contorted his body; an infection developed at the wound site despite the antibiotics; and Helen feared the boy was developing pneumonia.

Eventually, and in Helen's view through miraculous intervention, Kiran survived his ordeal. It took him many weeks to recover, but in time he returned home.

For almost four decades Helen Huston has served the sick and dying in an area that without her would have been bereft of any medical help. Lifelong dedication wasn't necessarily something she'd set out to accomplish. Instead, the biggest joy in life for Dr. Helen was the journey. And God, in His infinite wisdom, directed that journey where He chose.

Christian and secular watchdogs alike noticed Dr. Helen's work. She received an "honorary life membership in the Nepal Medical Association at Kathmandu, never before granted to a doctor from a foreign country. She was awarded the Outstanding Achievement Award by the University of Alberta Medical Alumni Association in 1978." She received an Honorary Doctor of Laws degree in 1984, also from the University of Alberta. She was the first recipient of the Hillary Foundation's Award for Humanitarian Service in 1991 and was named to the Order of Canada in 1994.

Today, the 53-bed hospital in Amp Pipal continues to provide medical care to anyone in need. Dr. Helen retired from her practice there in 1992, but in many ways her heart remains in the rolling hillsides and lush forests of Nepal.

CHAPTER FOURTEEN

Stephanie Dixon:
Nothing Is Impossible
(1984–)

The sound of cheering spectators is deafening as Stephanie Dixon takes her place at the starting position in one of the eight lanes at Saanich Commonwealth Place in Victoria, British Columbia. While her fellow swimmers loosen up by shaking their limbs and shifting weight from one foot to another, Stephanie's pre-swim routine is a little different. Although physical conditioning is paramount in becoming a successful athlete, it's the mental game that can make or break even the best of the best—something this psychology student from the University of Victoria knows only too well. A clear, goal-centred focus uncluttered by self-doubt, worry or concern of any kind is something Stephanie concentrates on as she waits for the sharp pop of the start-gun to sound.

Although a veteran to pool competition, Stephanie is competing in a different venue on this cool January weekend in 2004. Like the other swimmers at this meet, she's trying to make the finals for the Vancouver Island Championship, despite the physical differences between herself and her colleagues. And not once but twice that weekend, Stephanie would not only better the disabled world records in the 200- and 400-metre Individual Medley but she'd also qualify for that weekend's finals and pre-qualify for the Canadian Interuniversity Sport Championship— and she'd do it with only one leg.

WHEN STEPHANIE DIXON ENTERED THE WORLD ON FEBRUARY 10, 1984, in Brampton, Ontario, her parents couldn't have been more proud. Their little girl was pink and healthy and beautiful. Despite the fact that she was born with only one leg, she was never treated any differently than any other little girl. When, at the age of five, her doctor told her she'd never be able to ride a two-wheel bicycle, the strong-minded youngster knew she had to prove him wrong. While her parents stood by on the sidelines, Stephanie took her seat on a borrowed bike, manoeuvred herself to make the quick transition from balancing to pedalling and took off down the sidewalk. She immediately fell, but that didn't deter her; she hopped back on the bike and tried and tried again, until at last, bruised and battered, she conquered the two-wheeler.

Stephanie credits her parents with reinforcing her belief that nothing is impossible and that she is every bit as capable of achieving her goals as someone with two legs.

I'm different like anyone else...My disability may be a bit more visible than the average person's, but I will accomplish anything I put my mind to.

Her parents enrolled her in every sport and activity imaginable, from horseback riding and skiing to diving and gymnastics. Stephanie was introduced to the pool by the time she was two, and although it was her love for the sport that kept her swimming, it wasn't long before she and her coaches recognized her natural talent.

By the age of 13 she entered her first swim meet, and just three years later she faced the pressure of international competition of Olympic proportions at the 2000 Paralympic Games in Sydney, Australia. Despite her fortitude, her first swim at that meet was challenging, even for a determined, single-minded person like herself, and she admitted in a Women Warriors athlete's profile that she was nervous.

I started to doubt myself and lost my confidence...In the race I started out in front, but then girls started to pass me. My negative thoughts started to be all I could think of and I just wanted to give up. Then I suddenly remembered the words my mother said to me earlier about going out there and doing the best job I could do for that day. I also remembered that I never give up and I wasn't going to go down without a fight.

In the middle of her swim, with positive thoughts replacing those of self-doubt, Stephanie showed her true champion's nature and caught up with the swimmers that had passed her earlier, capturing the silver medal for her performance. She remained focused for the rest of the competition, garnering a total of five gold and two silver medals, along with five new world records for her efforts. Four years later, at the 2004 Paralympics in Athens, Greece, she repeated her strong performance in Sydney by capturing one gold, six silver and a bronze medal, leading her team with an eight-medal total.

The desire to beat all odds has kept Stephanie focused on her goals and has strengthened her resolve that nothing is impossible. And it's that same determination that has her not only wanting to compete in able-bodied competitions, but also has her working toward achieving her national time so that some day she might be the first physically challenged swimmer to compete in the able-bodied Olympics.

In an after-meet interview with Rich Cole of the University of Victoria Vikes that weekend in January 2004, where she competed against able-bodied athletes at Saanich Commonwealth Stadium, Stephanie said, "Everyone's different and therefore everyone has their weaknesses...Some athletes are taller, some are shorter. While I could be faster with another leg, I've learned to adapt and focus on my strengths like everyone else."

At the same time, she doesn't push herself to accomplish everything at once. Instead, she establishes her goals and tackles them one at a time, enjoying her accomplishments along the way.

At the age of 19, Stephanie was not only successful at the Paralympic events, she'd competed in a number of world championships, hauling home the hardware at these events as well. In 1999, she received the Jim Vipon Award, and in 2001 she was recognized as "Swimming/Natation Canada's female athlete of the year" for swimmers with disabilities. Stephanie was also awarded the King Clancy Award in 2001 for increasing public awareness about the potential of disabled people.

But perhaps the greatest accomplishment of Stephanie's young life is in the person she's become. While she still has many goals she wants to achieve in the pool, her strength of character, dedication and a simple belief in herself serve as examples for the legions of swimmers who come after her.

CHAPTER FIFTEEN

Shananditti:
A Voice for the Beothucks
(1801–1829)

She must have wondered, in the final days of her life, why she was the last one. A beautiful, young woman, tall and lean and full of life, she should have been thinking of marrying and raising a family. But that was impossible. There were no more of her kind to join with in life's journey. At the age of 29 she felt very old and alone. And it was thoughts of death now, not new life, that plagued her day and night.

As she sat at the estate of her caregiver, Shananditti's gaze frequently went to the forest, filling her with memories of a time when she sat with her family around the fire, took joy at the birth of a new baby or feasted after a successful deer hunt. Hers was a strong people. Proud. Peaceful. Trusting. Why then was she chosen to watch them all die?

THE VILLAGE REJOICED AT SHANANDITTI'S BIRTH IN 1801. THE Beothucks of Newfoundland's interior, or Red Indians as they were frequently referred to because of the red ochre oil they applied to their skin, were already a dying race when Shananditti entered the world. Only four villages remained at that time with fewer than 200 living Beothucks, so the birth of a child always spelled hope.

That hope was short-lived, however, as time and time again the Beothuck peoples were faced with brutal attacks from hunters, trappers and other white European settlers—something Shananditti witnessed many times in her short, fated life.

The Beothucks were traditionally hunter-gatherers. Shananditti frequently accompanied her mother, scouting the forests for berries and bird eggs. Her father and the other men in the village hunted deer and caribou for their meat and hides, and scoured the rivers and lakes and nearby Atlantic Ocean for fish, lobster and seal.

But the settlement of Newfoundland by the Europeans made even food gathering a dangerous occupation, something Shananditti experienced firsthand.

One morning she descended alone to the edge of the river to wash two pieces of venison. Suddenly a shot sounded from across the river. She felt a burning sensation in her leg and fell to the ground. On the opposite bank, she could see a white trapper reloading a long-barrelled musket. Frantically, she crawled up the bank. Another shot rang out and blood gushed from her hand. She struggled on and finally reached the safety of the trees and made her way back to the village.

This unprovoked attack wasn't unique. In Shananditti's short life she'd witness even more brutal and fatal confrontations. Death and destruction at the hands of the white men the Beothucks called *buggishaman* was all too common, and they did everything in their power to avoid confrontation with the newcomers.

It's no wonder, then, that any efforts on behalf of some Newfoundlanders who were genuinely concerned with the plight of the land's original inhabitants were often misunderstood. And it should come as no surprise that in 1807, when Governor John Holloway made a proclamation that monetary awards were offered for the capture of Beothucks, this caused even more violence. The idea, though meant to forge a relationship between the Red Indians and the *buggishaman*, instead induced terror when men who were protecting their wives and children were butchered and their wives taken captive.

Such was the fate of Shananditti's aunt, Demasduit, otherwise known as Mary March. On March 5, 1819, Shananditti watched as her uncle, Chief Nonosbawsut, was murdered because he tried to rescue his wife, Demasduit, from the clutches of Judge John Peyton Jr. His father, John Peyton Sr., and their delegation had been sent to "take some of the Indians and thus through them open a friendly communication with the rest." It was a brutal assault on a man doing everything in his power to protect his wife and losing his life in the process. And Shananditti witnessed every painful detail from the vantage point of a nearby wooded hill. It was the second time in as many years that Shananditti witnessed the murder of one of her own people, but it wouldn't be the last.

In March 1823, only Shananditti and five of her people were still alive—her uncle, a cousin, her parents and sister. They were suffering from starvation, and her uncle and cousin decided to make the dangerous journey to the coast to try their hand at hunting and fishing. Shananditti's father focused his efforts at hunting closer to home, but after waiting for several days for them all to return, Shananditti, her mother and sister decided to venture out themselves. They reasoned that their loved ones had been captured or murdered, and the women had given up all hope of maintaining any kind of traditional lifestyle. They were willing to give themselves up to the *buggishaman*.

As they made their way toward Badger Bay, the three women came upon the frozen bodies of Shananditti's uncle and cousin. Though not unexpected, it was a devastating blow.

For several weeks the women lived in a makeshift hut, surviving on a diet of blue mussels and birch bark, but they knew they couldn't continue to survive in this primitive way. They were cold, their hands numb and bleeding, and their diet insufficient to keep anyone alive for long.

They had to surrender. At that point they believed it would be better to be shot and killed by a white man's musket than to continue the slow, painful death they were experiencing.

Before too long they came upon a trapper, and they felt their fate was sealed. For there, standing just a few metres away with his musket raised and pointing in their direction, was William Cull—a man they knew as the ruthless murderer of Shananditti's mother's cousin. They knelt together waiting, believing their time had come, but what they didn't know was that the governor of Newfoundland had offered an award of 100 pounds sterling for the safe capture of the remaining few Beothucks. With far less effort than it would take to make this same wage in beaver pelts, Cull had hit pay dirt.

Still, Shananditti didn't leave the woods without witnessing one more brutal, deadly attack. As they were making their way to St. John's, the party came upon another trapper who was chasing a man "wearing a deerskin capote," and Shananditti recognized him. It was her father. He was still alive—but not for long.

As her father stood between two hunting parties, muskets raised in his direction, he knew his fate was sealed. But he wasn't going to let these men take his life, and in a split-second decision, he turned and ran across the thin ice of the nearby river, plunging into its icy depths.

There was no warning, no preliminary cracking noise, only a sudden splash of broken ice. Like a heavy brown stone, he sank beneath the surface. The trappers ran to the bank and pointed their muskets at the hole in the ice, waiting for his head to reappear. A cloud of mud swirled in the water, a few bubbles floated to the surface, and all was silent. After several minutes, the trappers lowered their weapons in disappointment. That was the last time Shananditti saw her father.

Although it seemed nothing equalling this tragedy could possibly threaten Shananditti and her two travelling companions, death visited twice more when Shananditti watched first her sister, then her mother, succumb to tuberculosis. Shananditti was truly alone.

Ironically, she ended up living as a servant in the Peyton's home on Burnt Island near the Bay of Exploits and was given the new name of Nancy April—like her aunt, Mary March, her last name indicated the month she was captured. For five years she cared for the Peyton children and performed household duties until world traveller and philanthropist, William Cormack, took an interest in this last-surviving Beothuck.

Being an educated man with a penchant for adventure, Cormack felt a unique kinship with the devastated race of people after his own excursion through Newfoundland's interior in 1822. It was because of his efforts that a society called the Beothuck Institute was formed "for the purpose of opening a communications with, and promoting the civilization of the Red Indians of Newfoundland." The society effectively raised awareness of this depleted peoples and at the same time was responsible for the support, care and education for Shananditti.

Thus, in a very short time, William Cormack accomplished what all before him had failed to do. He drew public attention to the Beothucks; he aroused the moral indignation of others "to do something for the sake of humanity"; he formed a society for the preservation of the Beothucks; he brought recognition of the unique value of Shananditti, and he launched a program of investigation into the Beothuck culture.

At this point in Cormack's involvement, it wasn't clear if there were any Beothuck survivors living in the wooded interior of Newfoundland. At least two expeditions went out to search for any survivors, but even with a substantial monetary incentive, none were found. In a last-ditch effort, Cormack conducted a search of his own. Accompanied by three First Nations guides from another tribe, Cormack descended into the interior. He found no surviving Beothucks, but he did discover a cache of artifacts, evidence of their hunting practices, and other important pieces in the puzzle of their history.

That no other Beothucks existed was something Shananditti already knew, but for Cormack, the reality that attempts to protect these peoples came too late left him distraught. It also reinforced the importance of working with Shananditti in devising a written history of the Beothucks in an effort to "communicate what would otherwise have been lost."

During the winter months of 1828 and 1829, Cormack and Shananditti worked tirelessly. A bright, talented woman who'd adapted to her new surroundings and even learned how to communicate in English, Shananditti was encouraged by Cormack to share her stories as he dutifully recorded them. Together, they devised a small dictionary of Beothuck words. And when he discovered Shananditti's ability to draw, Cormack encouraged her to create a pictorial history of her people.

Of their efforts, only a remnant has survived. Although it appears, through Cormack's writings, that Shananditti completed numerous sketches of her peoples, describing everything from their way of life to their hunting and fishing practices, only 10 remain. Of those 10, "five represent scenes from the closing history of Shananditti's people and five of religion. These drawings form a unique contribution to an important and neglected period in Canadian history."

As Cormack continued to record the Beothuck history, Shananditti relived the terror she had witnessed when her people were massacred and murdered. She explained how women bared their breasts to prove they weren't men. They begged for mercy, only to be shot and killed. Nevertheless, knowing hers was the last voice of a now extinct race, she persevered until her death from tuberculosis on June 6, 1829.

Having lived a life of tragedy, Shananditti's poor body could not even rest in peace after her death. Years later, the Church of England Cemetery where she was buried, on the south side of St. John's, was excavated to make way for a road.

"Even her bones are lost. Only her name endures. Shananditti: the last of the Beothucks."

CHAPTER SIXTEEN

Canadian Voice of Women for Peace:
A Voice for Our Future
(1960)

From the outset, the organization's philosophy has been one of inclusiveness and outreach to other women, refusing to accept labelling of other women as "enemy." They espouse and practice peace building through cooperation. Their record speaks of the mobilization of women, and public and governmental education.

–Rosalie Bertell

AMID THE RISING SMOKE THREATENING TO OVERCOME THEM as they hurry down a rain-drenched road, three children run. A boy, who looks to be about nine years old, leads the trio. He is terrified—you can tell by the tight lines on his face; his mouth is formed into a perpetual scream. The little girl to his left is about the same age. She's looking over her shoulder, perhaps seeking out the face of her mother or grandmother somewhere among the soldiers and others swarming nearby. The other girl is running naked. There was no time to dress. Perhaps she isn't even aware that she has no clothes. The only thing that matters to these children is that they escape the smoke, the smell and the destruction that threatens to overwhelm them.

Photographer Tim Page captured the image described above on June 8, 1972—perhaps the most famous surviving image of the Vietnam War. The scene was captured near Trang Bang, about 42 kilometres outside of Saigon, and the three Vietnamese children were fleeing their homes after a napalm bomb had been accidentally dropped on their village.

The Vietnam War was part of the Cold War and raged from 1957 to 1975, claiming more than 2 million civilian casualties and, although estimates vary, anywhere from one to 2.5 million dead. And it's precisely this kind of destruction that the Canadian Voice of Women for Peace has been speaking against for more than four decades.

Founded in 1960, the Canadian Voice of Women for Peace was initiated as a challenge by *Toronto Star* columnist Lotta Dempsey. In one of her articles, Dempsey asked women who were concerned about the fragile, political state of the world at the time, and who were willing to do something about the persistent threat of nuclear war, to write her. She likely didn't expect the response she received. Hundreds of women wrote in. Jo Davis, Dorothy Henderson, Helen Tucker and Beth Touzel teamed up with Dempsey, and they took the challenge a step further by forming the Voice of Women (later the Canadian Voice of Women for Peace).

The mandate of the new, voluntary non-partisan organization was to oppose "violence and war and promote disarmament and peace." By the end of their first year in operation, the group had acquired 6000 members.

The group developed a tactical plan of their own like generals in a war. But instead of using force, they used reason. They rallied together, organizing groups in every province of the country. They promoted ongoing educational campaigns, organized demonstrations, and continually lobbied governments around the world in their efforts to promote peace.

By the end of their first decade, the group had already approached the United Nations (UN) to declare an International Year of Peace, gained the attention of the Canadian government by pushing them to support a ban on nuclear testing and held demonstrations urging the end of the Vietnam War.

They continued their activism throughout the 1970s, and by 1977 the group was accredited with observer status at the UN. In the 1980s, provincial groups began making headlines, such as when the East Coast chapter voiced their opposition to their coastlines being used by U.S. nuclear warships for training exercises.

More recently, the Canadian Voice of Women for Peace issued a written statement offering their collective condolences to the victims of the terrorist attacks of September 11, 2001, while at the same time urging the U.S. government against retaliation.

We in Voice of Women recognize this point in time as a potentially transformative moment of great magnitude. There are critical choices to be made. In the midst of this great tragedy we see signs of hope as more and more people are coming to the realization that violent responses to violent attacks can only result in increased insecurity and instability and the deaths of more innocent people.

Today, the group that had formed from the mere germ of an idea, delivered by the impassioned pen of Lotta Dempsey, continues to grow and speak out against all forms of violence. Its collective voice joins with that of the little girl in the photograph described earlier. She was later identified as Phan Thi Kim Phuc, and 25 years after the bombing of her village, she was named to the United Nations Educational, Scientific and Cultural Organization (UNESCO) as a goodwill ambassador.

CHAPTER SEVENTEEN

Rene M. Caisse:
Essiac Inventor
(1888–1978)

*I have never claimed that my treatment cures
cancer—although many of my patients and the
doctors with whom I have worked claim that it
does. My goal has been control of cancer, and
alleviation of pain. Diabetes, pernicious anemia
and arthritis are not curable; but with insulin,
liver extract and adrenal cortex extracts, "incur-
ables" live out comfortable, controlled life spans.*

–Rene M. Caisse

RENE CAISSE WAS ALREADY A SEASONED MEDICAL PROFESSIONAL,
working as a head nurse in a northern Ontario
community, when she met a fascinating woman.
Noticing the scar tissue on the breast of this elderly
patient she was caring for, Rene asked the cause.

The woman explained that she had been diagnosed with advanced breast cancer many years
before, and doctors had wanted to remove her
breast. Prior to seeing these physicians, however,
this prospector's wife had met with a native medicine man living near the mining camp where she

and her husband were living. He, too, provided the same diagnosis, but with a different treatment. When she pondered her alternatives, she decided to revisit the medicine man before having the recommended surgery.

Pointing out a variety of naturally growing herbs, the medicine man then instructed her on brewing a tea. He told her to drink it every day—something she did from that time on until her hospital stay where she met Rene.

The woman's story got Rene thinking. "I knew that doctors threw up their hands when cancer was discovered in a patient; it was the same as a death sentence, just about. I decided that if I should ever develop cancer, I would use this herb tea."

Some time later, a casual visit with a physician friend reinforced the woman's story. He, too, explained, during a walk through his garden, that should people use a particular weed he pointed to, "there would be very little cancer in the world." It was the same plant that Rene's patient had confided saved her from her cancer.

Rene put these claims to the test when, just a few months later, her aunt went through surgery. Doctors declared the cancer that invaded her stomach and threatened her liver would claim her life in less than six months. With help from her aunt's doctor, Dr. R.O. Fisher—a man Rene herself had worked with throughout the years—Rene obtained the herbs and brewed the tea. Her aunt regained her strength and lived another 21 years, cancer free.

With one successful story under her belt, others soon followed. Repeatedly, patients were brought to Rene for her herbal remedy, which was either consumed as a brew or injected intramuscularly. These people recovered. Eventually, Rene set up a laboratory in the basement of her mother's home, and "she and Dr. Fisher began research on mice inoculated with human carcinoma." Through their research, they concluded that administering the remedy both intramuscularly and orally could work cooperatively for the benefit of the patient.

By giving the intramuscular injection in the forearm, to destroy the mass of malignant cells, and giving the medicine orally to purify the blood, I got quicker results.

It was an exciting time. Her research was going well, and doctors in the area were eager for her services. Rene and Dr. Fisher continued to refine the product until they isolated what they deemed was the herb responsible for reducing the tumours. The time had come to name their herbal remedy, and Rene chose the name Essiac—her surname spelled backwards. As for the identity of the herbs in this remedy, Rene kept that information to herself.

At one point, eight Toronto-area doctors approached Rene and asked her to concoct the brew for an elderly man whose face was being eaten away and who was experiencing dangerous blood loss. Doctor's didn't expect him to live another fortnight, but after Rene gave the man her tea, he stopped bleeding and survived another six months, only to die of pneumonia at Easter 1926.

The successful application of her remedy in this case spurred the eight doctors to sign a petition to the Department of National Health and Welfare at Ottawa, asking the government to consider financially supporting Rene's research.

I was joyful beyond words at this expression of confidence by such outstanding doctors regarding the benefits derived from my treatment. My joy was short-lived. Soon after receiving this petition, the Department of Health and Welfare sent two doctors from Ottawa to have me arrested for "practising medicine without a licence."

Rene wasn't arrested, but the visit was the beginning of almost 50 years of controversy between her, government officials and doctors not directly acquainted with her efforts. While she worked out of the Christie Street Hospital Laboratories in Toronto from 1928 to 1930, and even consulted with Dr. Frederick Banting of the Banting and Best duo who discovered insulin, she kept her formula to herself. She reasoned that because she wasn't a licensed physician, researching Essiac within the confines of a university setting could put her in jeopardy of losing any control over the development and subsequent use of her product.

I wanted to establish my remedy...in actual practice and not in a laboratory only. I knew it had no bad side effects, so it could do no harm. I wanted to use it on patients in my own way. And when the time came, I wanted to share in the administration of my own discovery.

Rene continued with her own investigations of Essiac, and the success of its treatment on terminally ill cancer patients seemed to reinforce her discovery. Meanwhile, a cancer commission was established in Ontario in an effort to sort out legitimate discoveries from the claims of charlatans. Between public hearings and political wrangling, Rene moved forward, eventually opening a clinic in her hometown of Bracebridge, Ontario.

The resultant "Cancer Clinic" was established at the old British Lion Hotel for $1 per month for rent, and it operated from 1934 to 1942. Rene was confident she'd eventually gather all the proof she needed to have Essiac declared an approved treatment by the medical profession. After all, she'd seen patients deemed hopeless cases by their doctors arrive by ambulance and leave on their own two feet time and time again. Surely the repeated success of her treatment would eventually call attention to the medical community at large.

After an onslaught of public pressure, in 1936 another petition was circulated throughout various Ontario communities. It was submitted to Health Minister Dr. Faulkner, Premier Hepburn and the Attorney General, stating:

Cancer is the greatest scourge of humanity...and therefore anyone who can cure it should be permitted and encouraged to do so. Wherefore, it be resolved that we very strongly urge that the Honourable Minister of Health fulfil his promise and have this treatment investigated in order that cancer sufferers be given a chance to recover their health.

Feeling the public pressure, Faulkner spoke with Dr. Banting at a meeting of the Canadian Medical Association. Together they devised an agreement whereby Rene could use the Banting Institute at the University of Toronto, offering her regular, weekday hours to conduct her research and no pressure to divulge Essiac's ingredients.

While this was a far sweeter offer than the one a few years earlier, Rene had become jaded by the medical profession. Nevertheless, interest from south of the border eventually had Rene making trips every other week to the Northwestern University Medical School in Chicago, Illinois, where, under the guidance of Dr. John Wolfer, she conducted clinical trials on terminal patients. She also travelled to the Mayo Clinic in Rochester, Minnesota, in an effort to do the same thing.

In the summer of 1937, a surgical specialist and coroner named Dr. Richard Leonardo of Rochester, New York, took an interest in Rene's work. And after spending several days going through clinical trials, Dr. Leonardo offered to set up a clinic there for her use. "I particularly appreciated Dr. Leonardo's opinion because he had been scientifically trained in Germany, Vienna, London and Scotland and he at first had been so completely sceptical of my treatment."

Despite Dr. Leonardo's attractive offer and another by Northwestern University to have a clinic set up there, Rene declined. She said she felt tied to her country and wanted it to be credited with any possible cancer cure.

Other sources, however, point to less positive results. In a letter to Dr. A. Moir of Peterborough, Ontario, Dr. Wolfer shared some doubts about the Chicago trials:

I'm sorry that there has been so much publicity about our clinic. The understanding was that when she began at our clinic, no publicity of any sort should be made…I fear that Miss Caisse is capitalizing the experience. Due to some personal contact about a year ago, Miss Caisse and her "Cure" were brought to my attention. Because of certain specifications that had been made, we thought it advisable to allow her to try her "Cure" on a limited number of cases.

The exact results of Rene's trials will likely never be known. Although she reported considerable success over the year and a half of travel to Chicago, other reports varied from positive to lukewarm to non-responsive. When Dr. Robert T. Nobel, the new registrar of the Ontario College of Physicians and Surgeons, wrote to Dr. Wolfer asking his opinion on the clinical trials conducted in Chicago, his response wasn't very supportive: "Miss Caisse came a number of times to the clinic and treated possibly eight or ten patients. In no case did we see any appreciable benefits."

In the following years, Rene suffered intense scrutiny. She did have supporters, but other doctors and researchers claimed her herbal remedy did nothing—and that patients who appeared to have been cured by it were either misdiagnosed or the treatment they received prior to receiving Essiac was to be credited for their return to health.

A year before her death in 1977, Rene Caisse and Essiac were the main focus of an article in the summer edition of *Homemakers Magazine*. Prior to its official release, copies of the magazine were "hand-delivered to various doctors and top government officials as a courtesy, and each contained a letter dated June 6 written by Executive Vice-President Jeffrey W. Shearer." The letter summarized the article and offered to open the research files accumulated by the magazine in preparation for the article. Shearer even offered to set up an interview with Rene, if anyone so desired. He received several responses to his letter, including this one:

I know of no acceptable ethical way for testing her compound in the absence of knowledge about the contents and possible toxicity. The evidence supporting her cure is, for the most part, anecdotal and couldn't be used in the study of the efficacy of the compound. It has been made very clear…that if she will provide information about the contents there are ways of testing its usefulness.

I would doubt that she will change her attitude at the age of 88, but maybe her heirs will be willing to listen to reason.

It's unfortunate that Rene Caisse didn't accept Dr. Banting's offer of a research facility earlier in her fight to gain recognition for Essiac. It is only through appropriately conducted clinical trials that any kind of concrete claims of a drug's merit can be made. However, Rene's dedication to the care and cure of cancer patients in the face of all adversity and the years she spent researching Essiac and treating cancer patients without ever charging for her services, was more than merely commendable.

Essiac is still being marketed as an herbal supplement, and there are those who swear by its healing powers. Though Altramed Health Products Inc., sponsors of a website reviewing *The History of Essiac and Rene Cassie, Canada's Cancer Nurse*, clearly states that "it is illegal to claim that Essiac can cure anything. It is sold only as an herbal dietary supplement."

CHAPTER EIGHTEEN

Geraldine Moodie:
Framing History
(1854–1945)

The flies were unbelievably hungry that warm August day as Geraldine Moodie lay on her belly beside a patch of wild columbine. Camera in hand and flowers framed just so, she waited for the exact moment when the sun would catch their yellow centres, highlighting the contrast between them and their ruby red crowns. She'd been waiting some time, and despite the bug bites she'd tolerated, she was happy to do so. After all, contrast was everything in black-and-white photography. And with a little patience, maybe a humming bird would happen along and it too would find itself immortalized for all time to come.

GERALDINE FITZGIBBON WAS BORN IN TORONTO, ONTARIO, on October 31, 1854. A strong-willed youngster, Geraldine appeared to be a bit of a challenge for her famous aunt, Catherine Parr Traill. Her equally famous grandmother, Susanna Moodie, however, was quite taken by the child she'd nicknamed "Cherry." In a letter to her British publisher,

Susanna described her granddaughter during a visit with her convalescing mother:

A beautiful delicate little sprite of a child, or "frairy," as my Irish maids called her, who believed that she must be something super human as she was born at midnight, on All Hallow eve, and was so small and clever, and so lovely. I never saw such a tiny creature walking and talking, and with a face of such bright intelligence...when she left us Madam Cherry, had rosy cheeks and sparkling eyes and was full of fun and frolic and vitality.

Geraldine's lawyer father, Charles Thomas Fitzgibbon, died when she was just a youngster of 11, leaving Agnes Dunbar Moodie, Geraldine's mother, with the daunting task of caring for six small children.

An illustrator of considerable ability, Agnes was commissioned by Susanna and Catherine to illustrate Catharines book, *Canadian Wild Flowers,* in an effort to help Agnes earn money for her family. It was an endeavour assisted by Geraldine, who was developing into an artist in her own right, and the experience opened a world of creativity to the young girl.

There's not much information on whether Geraldine pursued her love of art much before she was married. She met her husband, a distant cousin by the name of John Douglas Moodie, during an extended trip to England to visit a great aunt. The two were married on June 8, 1878, and for a time lived with John's parents. The couple welcomed their firstborn, daughter Melville Mary, in March 1879 while still living in England, and that same fall Geraldine returned to Canada with her new family and her father-in-law George, following the death of his wife Mary.

Although Geraldine's family settled in Eastern Canada, the West beckoned, and they tried their hand at homesteading near Brandon, Manitoba. For the next few years Geraldine busied herself with Melville and then the birth of George in 1882 and Alex in 1884. She also dabbled in her art again, sketching and painting the prairie wildflowers. Evening Primrose, Golden Bean, Shooting Star, Larkspur and others were individually composed with careful, gentle strokes—they looked so real you could almost catch their scent. The collection of watercolours she completed during this time was eventually exhibited at the Colonial and Indian Exhibition in London, England, in 1886. Geraldine's interest in capturing the essence of living things captivated her for the rest of her life.

By 1885 the Moodies moved off the farm, and John secured a position with the North-West Mounted Police (NWMP). Throughout his 22 years on the force, the Moodies were stationed in several Western Canadian communities, affording Geraldine a wide range of subjects to photograph. But it wasn't until their posting in the Battlefords that Geraldine began seriously focusing on her photography as a business. She opened her first studio in

July 1895, and in the process, became one of the
first women in Canada to accomplish this feat.
(English-born Hannah Matherly Maynard is
recorded as having established a photographic studio in Victoria, BC, in 1962.)

While family portraits represented a fair amount
of her workload, Geraldine was a shrewd historian, capturing images of the First Nations peoples
and the NWMP. In a letter to her Aunt Catherine,
Geraldine shared her enthusiasm:

*I have not seen much of the Indians this spring. I have
several promises to come and sit for their pictures when
I get my new studio and fixtures finished…It is very fascinating work and I can make enough to pay expenses
and something over when I fill all the orders I have…Some
of the views about Battleford are very pretty and will
make lovely pictures. There are some pretty bits about
20 miles out. Scenes of some of the fights during the
Rebellion of 1890 [sic] which I think will interest people
out east.*

Geraldine was obviously a gentle soul whose
energy was infectious. She also managed to instil
a sense of confidence in her subjects. Not only did
she capture images of great Cree chiefs and young
warriors in her studio, she was permitted to take
photos of sacred ceremonies, such as the Sun
Dance, and personal images of the Native peoples
at home and in their villages. They obviously
trusted her, and it's to history's benefit that they
did, as her collection provides a particularly

detailed look at their lives and their culture from a woman's perspective.

Geraldine's self-confidence was especially evident when, ignoring all protocol of the day that would have a woman behave in a considerably less-forward fashion, she captured photographs of Prime Minister Sir Mackenzie Bowell during a 1895 visit to the Battlefords. It was a move that apparently gained her Bowell's recognition because she landed a commission that same year to "photograph historic sites and other areas visited" by the prime minister.

Extremely inventive when it came to making money with her photography, Geraldine understood the need to diversify and offer different products to her customers. One such product was specially designed Christmas and New Year cards which, according to the *Saskatchewan Herald*, were so popular that its advertisements warned consumers to place orders early so as not to be disappointed when they were no longer available.

By the time the Moodies moved to Maple Creek, Saskatchewan, in 1896, Geraldine had earned the reputation of being a top-rated photographer. In the following spring, she opened a studio in Maple Creek and branched out to open a second studio in Medicine Hat, Alberta, some 97 kilometres west. With six children at home by that time, Geraldine hired domestic help to allow her the freedom to travel between the two locales, sometimes staying in Medicine Hat for two weeks at a time to take pictures before returning home to develop them.

She did well in this venture for a time, but as word spread that a lone woman had cornered the market in not one but two communities, it wasn't long before she had competition. She closed her Medicine Hat business in 1897 and focused all of her energies in Maple Creek. While John was away for a 15-month stint mapping an overland route to the Yukon from Edmonton, Geraldine did portrait work. She also maintained her interest in wildflowers, documenting, illustrating and photographing the variety of species in her area. And she steadfastly chronicled life on the prairies at that time, capturing images of cattle round-ups, cowboys branding the cattle, parades, school photos and local sports teams—wherever life was happening, Geraldine was sure to be there, camera in hand.

In 1903, John was promoted to superintendent and assigned to Hudson Bay and the Eastern Arctic regions. Geraldine and their youngest son Alex followed him the next year. When Geraldine arrived at her destination of Fullerton Harbour on Southampton Island, living arrangements were still under construction for the officers and the lone, non-Inuit woman among them. As a result, Geraldine and Alex lived in the steamship *The Arctic*, which brought them across the northern waters to their new home, until their new residence was built.

Understandably, it took Geraldine time to adjust to her new environment. The North was a cold, isolated, lonely place for a woman used to the finer things in life. Despite the fact the Department of Marine and Fisheries had already secured an official photographer in the person of Frank McKean, it wasn't long before Geraldine documented her new experience with as much attention to detail and enthusiasm for life as she had before.

It was another first for Canadian women, as Geraldine was the first to capture images of Inuit culture at that time in Canada's history, and her photographs are said to be some of the best in existence. In fact, it was because she was a woman that her images portrayed a different side of Inuit life that her male counterparts may not have found as interesting at the time. Not only did she photograph the frozen landscape, the steamships arriving and leaving Fullerton Harbour, the Inuit on their whaling ships and women ice fishing, she was also enthralled by the people, their expressions, their clothing. A large selection of the portraits show women in their beaded Attigi (traditional leather garments), women with faces tattooed in a marriage ritual, mothers and their children, men with seal harpoons—the images record a way of life that obviously touched Geraldine both as an artist and as a woman.

The Moodies stayed in the North for a little over a year before returning south for a time, but by August 1906 they returned to Churchill, where for the next three years Geraldine would continue exploring the northern way of life through her photography. She also extensively catalogued plant life in the area, climbing rocks and searching crevices for just the right specimen.

While waiting to hear about their next posting, and in between smaller assignments John was given, Geraldine continued with her photography. The couple was hoping for another position in the North. Instead, John was put in charge of the Regina district from 1910 to 1912 until he was transferred, this time to Dawson in the Yukon Territory. From 1915, John had a series of shorter assignments, and Geraldine accompanied him on some of these trips. He retired in 1917, and the couple settled for a time back in Maple Creek, where John served as a justice of the peace and the town's coroner.

In 1936, the Moodies moved to Duncan, BC, and lived with their daughter Melville, her husband and their extended family. Sadly, most of Geraldine's negatives were confused with items being shipped to a second-hand store and were lost. Hopefully, with time, they will be rediscovered.

Geraldine continued to take photos and develop her negatives into her 80s when, having lost her vision in one eye, she decided to develop her prints commercially. The couple moved to Calgary in 1944. Geraldine died a year later, and John passed away in 1947.

CHAPTER NINETEEN

Barbara Frum:
Queen of the Airwaves
(1937–1992)

*I hate falseness…I hate a lie—the big ones as well
as the little tiny ones…and that really fuels me.*

–Barbara Frum

HER MOTHER'S FORESIGHT WAS PERHAPS THE FIRST CLUE THAT
Barbara Frum would be a pioneering woman in
her own right. Florence Rosenberg, an American-
born woman, demonstrated her own pioneering
spirit by bucking the trend of the day and, even
though she was a woman, attained a university
degree. She'd opted to have her daughter in the
U.S. so that Barbara would benefit from having an
American passport, and Barbara was born in Nia-
gara Falls, New York, on September 8, 1937.

As a young adult, Barbara hadn't really thought
about a career. In 1957 she married her childhood
sweetheart, Murray Frum, and after completing a
Bachelor of Arts degree at the University of
Toronto, had her first son, David, and settled down
to life as a wife and a mother. Linda and Matthew
came along soon after.

I was happy as a clam…Nobody can believe it. I was blissfully happy, just completely enchanted with being a mother and taking care of that child and entertaining friends and going out to dinner. I had never thought about a job. I was heading into being a very scientific wife and mother. That's what my mother had done. I read, I studied, I intellectualized what my child was doing. I felt that what I was doing was really worthwhile. And I was very good at it.

Barbara's entry into the world of journalism was initiated by an article she wrote for the *Toronto Star* on behalf of a charity for which she was a volunteer. By 1963 she was earning $35 a week as the host of the CBC radio show *Matinee*. The show's focus was on helping mothers amuse their youngsters—something Barbara admittedly loved doing with her own. But she wanted more, and her big break likely came about when she broke the story of corruption surrounding the TB seals campaign, a story that also appeared in the *Toronto Star*. Within two years of its publication, she was working as a full-time journalist.

Still, despite her obvious talent and intelligence, Barbara's quick wit and cutting edge often put her at odds with her employers. In 1971 she was fired from the CBC's Toronto public affairs show *Weekday* because management considered her questions "too tough."

However, it was these same qualities that drew the attention of other radio executives who were looking to develop something a little more hard-hitting on their play list, and by the fall of 1971 she was asked to host *As It Happens*.

People who wanted information and a national voice on Canadian and international affairs were ready to be lured back to radio. The show...was deliberately designed to break all the old, safe CBC rules. The orders were: provide an iconoclastic, zippy, nightly information package. Speak to everybody, not just to the few who genuflect to the sound of a mid-Atlantic accent.

And that's exactly what she did—for 10 years and "$2,100 worth of dimes a week" Barbara dialed for interviews around the world. Although phone-in shows weren't unique to radio by 1971, phoning-out was. It wasn't long before efforts to turn around the traditional lull after the 6:00 PM news bore results. *As It Happens*—a mix of the most important news of the day from around the world and the quirkiest stories that seemed to be pure fiction—tantalized listeners everywhere and grew in popularity. It was everything and more than CBC executives could have hoped for.

It was also a daily challenge that fuelled her 12- and 14-hour shifts with the energy she needed to get to the bottom of yet another amazing story.

With every interview, Barbara's conversation seemed effortless, and the magic of radio made it appear to the listener as though the world was really just a phone call away—all you had to do was dial the number.

But it wasn't like that. Barbara arrived at the studio six or eight hours before air time to interview guests and organize the day's stories. And whether that night's line-up was par for the course or out of this world largely depended on luck.

In one case, dissension erupted over fishing territory between the Icelanders and Britain in what was coined the "Cod War," resulting in a group of Icelanders stoning the British embassy. *As It Happens*, always attempting to live up to its namesake, decided to telephone the embassy to see if they could get comment from the British ambassador.

Within minutes, Barbara found herself talking to the man himself—and he wasn't too pleased. Apparently, the phone call from CBC had tied up the only available line, and the British ambassador hadn't even notified his own government of the situation.

Barbara persisted, reminding the ambassador that if he just agreed to answer one question she'd happily get off the line. He relented. "And that's how *As It Happens* listeners that night got to hear the views of a besieged British diplomat with the sound of his own embassy being stoned in the background."

In her book, *As It Happened*, Barbara shares the roller-coaster ride of life as a journalist. As host of the show from 1971 to 1981, Barbara's eclectic and strong interviewing style had her speaking with everyone from prime ministers and members of royalty to Sandra Good of the Manson gang.

Her questions were penetrating, and her mind was clear and sharp. Barbara Frum was not only an inspiration for aspiring women journalists everywhere, she was a formidable force against the most cynical, hard-nosed guest.

Such was the case during her now infamous interview in March 1979 with Harold Ballard, owner of the Toronto Maple Leafs. Barbara was navigating a three-way conversation between herself, Ballard, and Dick Beddoes, a columnist with Toronto's *Globe and Mail*. Throughout the interview, Ballard didn't hide the contempt he felt for women on the radio.

"Who needs women on the radio anyways—they're a joke," he said, directing his comments to Beddoes. "You know where they're good...You know where they're their best, don't you?"

Barbara didn't flinch. She maintained her poise and good manners, despite Ballard's constant quips, right to the end of the interview when, after she asked a question, Ballard hung up on her. Not exactly known for his good graces, Ballard's comments nonetheless reinforced his image as rough, outrageous and sexist—and Barbara's image as a woman who could maintain her composure with just about anyone.

Barbara particularly liked the immediacy of the show's phone-out format. When a Greenwich Village bank in New York City was being held up by a bank robber named "Cat," the CBC was the first to capture a live interview with the perpetrator, thanks to Ma Bell.

"We got the branch's number from the bank's head office and cut right by the army of battle-dressed policemen sealing off the area—right into the bank. The phone rang once, twice, a third time. Then a cheerful male voice came on the line."

It seemed the culprit was quite happy with the chance to air his views on Canadian radio. When asked what was happening, he explained he had 11 hostages and was negotiating for "Patty Hearst, the Harris', and that oriental girl, plus 10 million in gold. That's it." Without another word he hung up, but by then CBC listeners had as much information as the policemen mediating the situation.

And then there were those stories that brought out the lighthearted side of life—those quirky, stranger-than-fiction encounters with people you'd only ever read about. Such was the case of her most requested interview with the British farmer who claimed to have grown a giant cabbage that was five feet (1.5 metres) in diameter. The idea of talking to a record-breaking cabbage-growing farmer must have seemed interesting enough, as far as quirky stories go. But the hard-of-hearing guest had a difficult time following Barbara's questions—his quick stop at a neighbourhood pub before the interview didn't help his comprehension any.

While Barbara kept asking what he'd fed his cabbage to make it grow so large, the British farmer kept offering to send her a photo. In the end, the only admission the farmer made was that he frequently spoke Gaelic to the leafy green *Brassica* growing in his garden. Perhaps that helped? In any case, the across-Atlantic encounter turned into one of the most humorous interviews of Barbara's career and the program's history.

By 1982 Barbara made her foray back into television with CBC's revamped national newscast *The Journal*. Barbara would later say that leaving *As It Happens* was like "getting a divorce from myself." And despite the concerns of CBC executives that she may not be able to make the transition from radio to television, the show went on to be another big success for CBC, garnering about 2.5 million viewers nightly.

Weeknights for 10 years, Canadians welcomed Barbara into their living rooms. Now, when faced with cantankerous characters like Harold Ballard, fans not only heard Barbara's composure, they saw it.

Initially, Barbara co-hosted the program with fellow journalist Mary Lou Finlay until producer Mark Starowicz decided the show was too short to justify two hosts. By the time *The Journal* had aired for two years, Mary Lou had moved to a field position and Barbara remained as the sole host.

As a woman working in what was then still a mostly male-dominated profession, Barbara's most formidable interview was, ironically, with another strong-minded woman like herself. Canada's Queen of the Airwaves was up against Britain's Iron Lady, Margaret Thatcher. The two women went head-to-head on public policy decisions. Barbara delved into the particulars of the British prime minister's answers, and Thatcher tried to put Barbara in her place. The interview was a tense one, with neither woman willing to back down from her respective stance. Starowicz would later comment that the two women had taken an instant dislike to each other.

An interview that touched Barbara perhaps like no other was her meeting with Nelson Mandela just days after his release from 27 years in a South African prison. Sitting behind Mandela's home in Soweto township with the sound of birds chirping and the gentle, wafting breeze counteracting the hot sun if only just a little, the two sat, facing each other, in candid conversation. Although Barbara initially balked at the idea of interviewing the South African hero, she later called this "one of the most important encounters of her career."

Barbara's last interview on *The Journal* was on March 10, 1992. Her guest was author Mordecai Richler. She didn't look herself. Her usual spark, that edge she had to every interview she tackled, wasn't quite there. Richler, obviously concerned for her well-being, broke the flow of the interview to ask if she was okay.

It was no wonder she hadn't appeared to have her usual edge. A trip to the hospital after the interview resulted in Barbara being admitted with a fever of 103°F. She died 16 days later.

Her death was a shock to the nation. The fact that this brave, strong woman had been fighting leukemia for the last 18 years of her life was something only a few, select people knew. She didn't want to be defined by her illness. And she wasn't going to be held prisoner by it either.

Four years after her mother's death, Linda Frum, in a television interview with Hana Gartner, remembered the life of a woman who'd inspired a nation. Linda had just published a memoir on her mother's life, *Barbara Frum: A Daughter's Memoir*. Linda reinforced the belief that her mother was driven by her work, but that she also lived for her family.

My mother habitually did three things at once. Her days…by choice and necessity…were relentless. By filling her day with so much, my mother was able to con all of us into the reassuring illusion that her leukemia was under control, and that she was not dying.

Linda explained how her mother "did everything intensely," from her work as a journalist to her life as a wife and mother to her love for her dog, Diva. Linda even suggested, after reports from one doctor and then another didn't give her mother much hope for surviving more than a year or two with her condition, a diagnosis of leukemia was partly responsible for her living life to its fullest. Just as she wouldn't give in to being bullied in an interview, Barbara wouldn't give in to death. It would come when it did. And, as she'd often say to her family, there was "no point in dying a thousand deaths—you should only have to die once."

In the end, she died as she had lived—with a blend of wit, hope and faith, and dignity enough for all.

Notes on Sources

General References
http://dictionary.reference.com/
Merna Forster. *100 Canadian Heroines: Famous and Forgotten Faces*. Toronto, ON: Dundurn Press, 2004.
Louise Arbour
Carol Off. *The Lion, The Fox, and The Eagle*. Random House Canada, 2000.
http://www.cbc.ca/news/background/arbour/
http://en.wikipedia.org/wiki/Louise_Arbour
http://en.wikipedia.org/wiki/Slobodan_Milosevic
Anne Campbell
Anne Campbell. *Dr. Anne Adamson Campbell, ARCT, LMus.*, OC, autobiography, 1999.
Canadian Voice of Women for Peace
http://www.vietnampix.com/
http://home.ca.inter.net/~vow/
Rene Caisse
Donna M. Ivey. *Clinic of Hope: The Story of Rene M. Caisse and Essiac*. Toronto, ON: Dundurn Press, 2004.
http://www.essiacinfo.org/
Stephanie Dixon
http://www.caaws.ca/olympics/2004/paralympic_sports/swimming/sept_25.cfm
http://www.womenwarriors.ca/en/athletes/profile.asp?id=7
http://ring.uvic.ca/04oct07/features/
The Famous Five
Nancy Millar. *The Famous Five: Emily Murphy and the Case of the Missing Persons*. Cochrane, AB: The Western Heritage Centre, 1999.
http://www.collectionscanada.ca/famous5/index-e.html
Muriel McQueen Fergusson
http://www.moondance.org/1997/autumn97/nonfiction/muriel.html
http://epe.lac-bac.gc.ca/100/200/301/nlc-bnc/celebrating_women-ef/women97/emcqueen.htm
Barbara Frum
Barbara Frum. *As It Happened*. Toronto, ON: McClelland and Stewart, 1976.
Myrna Kostash, Melinda McCracken, Valerie Miner, Erna Paris & Heather Robertson. *Her Own Woman: Profiles of Ten Canadian Women*. Toronto, ON: The Macmillan Company of Canada, 1975.
http://archives.cbc.ca/300i.asp?id=1-74-368
http://www.cbc.ca/lifeandtimes/frum.html
http://radio.cbc.ca/programs/ideas/shows/frum/
Helen Huston
Gerald W. Hankins, M.D. *A Heart For Nepal: The Dr. Helen Huston Story*. Winnipeg, MB: Windflower Communications, 1992.
http://collections.ic.gc.ca/heirloom_series/volume6/226229.htm
http://www.lieutenantgovernor.ab.ca/aoe/huston.cfm
Silken Laumann
Steve McLean. Silken's New Challenge. *Toronto Sun*, July 24, 2004.
Jim Slotek. Silken's Story. *Toronto Sun*, June 23, 1996.

George Gross. Silken's Story, Step by Step. *Toronto Sun*, August 12, 1992.
Christie Blatchford. Silken: Class and Courage. *Toronto Sun*, August 3, 1992.
http://www.collectionscanada.ca/women/002026-232-e.html
http://www.canoe.ca/OlympicsCanadaLaumann/home.html
http://www.silkensactivekids.com/

Dorothy Livesay

Dorothy Livesay. *Journey with My Selves, A Memoir 1909-1963*. Vancouver, BC:
    Douglas & McIntyre Ltd., 1991.
Dorothy Livesay. *The Self-Completing Tree*. Victoria, BC: Press Porcepic Ltd., 1986.
Peter Stevens. *Dorothy Livesay, Patterns in a Poetic Life*. Toronto, ON: ECW
    Press, 1992.
Paul Denham. *Dorothy Livesay and Her Works*. Toronto, ON: ECW Press, 1987.

Flora MacDonald

Alvin Armstrong, *Flora MacDonald*. Don Mills, ON: J.M. Dent & Sons (Canada)
    Limited, 1976.
http://www.the-south-asian.com/Aug2004/Flora%20MacDonald.htm

Geraldine Moodie

Donny White. *In Search of Geraldine Moodie*. Regina, SK: Canadian Plains
    Research Center, University of Regina, 1998.

Anne Murray

Barry Grills. *Snowbird: The Story of Anne Murray*. Kingston, ON: Quarry Press,
    1996.
David Livingstone. *Anne Murray: The Story So Far*. Scarborough, ON: Prentice-
    Hall Canada Inc., 1982.
http://www.annemurray.com/
http://www.publicairwaves.ca/index.php?page=845

Marion Orr

http://www.histori.ca/minutes/minute.do?ID=10216
http://www.canadian99s.org/articles/p_orr.htm
http://www.airtransportaux.org/history.html

Shananditti

Susan E. Merritt. *Her Story: Women from Canada's Past*. St. Catharines, ON:
    Vanwell Publishing Ltd., 1993.
Keith Winter. *Shananditti: The Last of the Beothucks*. North Vancouver, BC:
    J.J. Douglas Ltd., 1975.

Charlotte Ross

Fred Edge. *The Iron Rose: The Extraordinary Life of Charlotte Ross, M.D.* Winnipeg,
    MB: University of Manitoba Press, 1992.

Mary Walsh

http://www.cbc.ca/lifeandtimes/walsh.html
http://www.collectionscanada.ca/women/002026-615-e.html
http://www.museum.tv/archives/etv/W/htmlW/walshmary/walshmary.htm

Charlotte Whitton

P.T. Rooke & R.L. Schnell. *No Bleeding Heart: Charlotte Whitton, A Feminist on
    the Right*. Vancouver, BC: UBC Press, 1987.
http://archives.cbc.ca/400i.asp?IDCat=73&IDDos=310&IDCli=1631&IDLan=
    1&type=inoubliable

~∞~